Burden of Ashes

Burden of Ashes

j u s t i n   c h i n

alyson books
los angeles | new york

MANUFACTURED IN THE UNITED STATES OF AMERICA.

THIS TRADE PAPERBACK ORIGINAL IS PUBLISHED BY ALYSON PUBLICATIONS,
P.O. BOX 4371, LOS ANGELES, CALIFORNIA 90078-4371.
DISTRIBUTION IN THE UNITED KINGDOM BY TURNAROUND PUBLISHER SERVICES LTD.,
UNIT 3, OLYMPIA TRADING ESTATE, COBURG ROAD, WOOD GREEN,
LONDON N22 6TZ ENGLAND.

FIRST EDITION: MAY 2002

02 03 04 05 06 **a** 10 9 8 7 6 5 4 3 2 1

ISBN 1-55583-642-9

COVER DESIGN BY MATT SAMS.
COVER PHOTOGRAPHY BY TONY STONE.

TO MY PARENTS AND MY BROTHER
"...MY VERSION..."

AND IN MEMORIAM TO MY TWO EXCEPTIONAL
GRANDMOTHERS

Contents

◊

ACKNOWLEDGMENTS

For financial assistance in completing this work, the author gratefully acknowledges the San Francisco Art Commission's Cultural Equity Grants Program.

Some of the writings in this book first appeared, in slightly different versions, in the following magazines, journals, Web zines, and anthologies: ZYZZYVA, *Harrington Gay Men's Fiction Quarterly*, *modern words*, *Urbanus*, *Prosodia*, *Big Bridge*, *The James White Review*, *Hawaii Review*, *Queer 13*, *Men on Men 5*.

The author also wishes to thank, for all-round goodness, general support, friendship, and other stuff, Dave Thomson, Lisa Asagi, Zack Linmark, DeCat, Morgan Blair, Richard Labonte, Lori Takayesu, Brighde Mullins, and Scott Brassart and the staff at Alyson.

Jagged

There is an old children's rhyme about an old, old house which had an old, old room. And in that old, old room was an old, old wardrobe; and in the old, old wardrobe was an old, old drawer; and in the old, old drawer was an old, old box; and in the old, old box was a ghost. The trick in telling the story was to keep lowering one's voice with each older smaller container, luring the listening to lean in. And when it is finally time to reveal the contents of the box, the rhyme-teller shouts "Ghost!" startling the listener—as if it were that little ghost inside the old box that was doing the spooking. But even if there was an actual ghost that was doing the spooking, what fear could such a little apparition, so small that it fits in a box that fits into a drawer, provoke in anyone? Still, when told just right, the little rhyming prank produced much merriment and laughter.

Somehow, I have remembered this little ditty all these years.

In Primary One (first grade), transferred midyear to a new school and put in the only available slot, I found myself in the slow class. One day, after correctly labeling the parts of a dog (head, tail, mouth, eye, leg, neck, body) and a fish (tail, fin, head, eye, gills), and while the rest of the class was still trying to figure out what was what, I was sent to the Art Room. The art teacher unfurled a large sheet of yellow cardboard paper in front of me and opened a box of broken blunt crayons. I was instructed to draw a big spooky haunted old house. I took my pencil and carefully traced the outlines of the house. It was on a steep cliff, and it leaned and sheared off in all wacky directions. There were giant cobwebs in all the impossibly shaped polygonal windows, and twisted chimneys with bats flying out of them. A big yellow full moon shone behind one of those chimneys. And the house was dark. Black, gray and brown and purple. The teacher was pleased with my artwork, and she cut out the picture of the house and attached it to wooden sticks. This was going to be used in the year-end variety show as the old, old house that held the room, the wardrobe, the drawer, the box, and the ghost.

In my toy cupboard at home sits a small Tupperware. Translucent, oblong, about the size of a Christmas fruitlog, the Tupperware used to hold six bars of Lux soap, a free gift for buying those bars of soap. No soapy Lux fragrance lingers in the tub anymore—for years it did, but it hasn't for even more years since. Still, in my mind I detect a faint familiar smell when I open the tub. The container stores the pieces of a 3,000-piece jigsaw puzzle. Not that there are 3,000 pieces anymore; a great number of pieces have gone missing, disappeared into the great unknown, eaten by pets and idiot cousins, lost under carpets and sofas, swept away in weekly house cleanings, filched by ghosts and goblins.

The jigsaw puzzle was given to an aunt as a Christmas present many, many years ago, when I was not even in kindergarten yet. It was, of course, an utterly fashionable, extravagant, absurd, and completely useless gift. For who had the time, the patience, or the bother to put the thing together? So the box fell to my brother and me. And what did we know of putting together a jigsaw puzzle? The box sat in the cupboard for years.

One holiday my cousins came to visit, and on a lazy afternoon, sitting in the air-conditioned room to escape the sweltering equatorial sun, we decided to do the jigsaw. We studied the picture on the box to help us decipher the pieces and put them in the correct order. It was a difficult one. The picture was that of a sunny scene on a jetty. There were lovers walking hand in hand along the railings, a woman in '60s-style glasses reading a book on a bench, roller skaters on the promenade. In the distance, there was a building that looked like an old church. There was a large cloudy sky with three different shades of blue. In the foreground were loads of foliage with red and yellow flowers, and a thick grove of palm trees whose peeling, husky trunks were difficult to tell apart.

We split the picture into several sections and each of us tackled our assigned section. The jigsaw lay on the floor for a full day and a full night, and the next day, in the afternoon, we finally put the last piece of the puzzle into place. We gathered to look at our finished work; then, in a childish shriek, we jumped onto the puzzle with our bare feet, crumbling it back into its 3,000 pieces.

My mother found the Tupperware in the storeroom, and the box with the original photo was thrown out.

Every year, for a few years after that, all through my primary school years, my cousins, friends, and I would put the puzzle together during my return home for semester break. Each of us became experts in one particular section. Mine was the foreground of foliage dotted with red and yellow flowers; my brother was a whiz at the jetty scene. We could piece together our sections with relative ease and in no time at all. We could look at any piece from our section and recognize where it went and what pieces fit around it.

But how much can jigsaw puzzles hold the fleeting wonder of children? Newer, more exciting board games occupied our interest, electronic games marveled us, bicycles promised freedom, ball games in the yard became king. Soon the Tupperware, with its soap fragrant scent perfuming those cardboard pieces, receded into the toy cupboard, chucked behind even more useless and boring toys like the scuba-diving flippers, the magic tricks set, and the children's mah-jongg game.

A few years ago, while visiting my parents, I dug into the

back of the toy cupboard looking for some old comics and I came across the Tupperware. Besotted with ennui and peppered with nostalgia—a most potent combination—I decided to try piecing the puzzle together.

I emptied the tub on the floor and started. It had been more than 20 years since anyone had done the puzzle. In my childhood, I always loved stories about how toys came to life and had adventures of all sorts. I imagined this poor tragic jigsaw, crying its sad tears, lying in ruins for so long, waiting for the day of redemption when it would be put together so that it could come to life and escape out the window in search of its one true lost love—only to be overcome by the rains, the flies, and, finally, some paper-eating mammal that lived in the swamps. So tragic.

I worked tirelessly for hours, determined to complete the puzzle, even though I knew what the picture was and, surprisingly, even remembered it so vividly.

Eventually the puzzle was completed. I leaned back and looked at the whole, and wondered where this place, with all its missing spots, was. We had all assumed it was Penang Island, in the northern part of Malaysia. We had gone there years ago for my father's high school reunion. We thrilled at taking the giant ferry across the channel; the second time we went back, the bridge traversing the channel had already been built, and traveling across that was a thrill too.

I wondered when the photo was taken. It must have been in the late '60s, I deduced; the clothes and the fashions gave that away. I wondered who these people were.

Did they know their photo was being taken? That they were going to be part of this puzzle? What sort of lives have they led? What was the woman on the bench reading, and where is she now? Probably dead. Palm and coconut trees survive a long time, and I wondered if there was something of the landscaping that still remained. Then again, I did not even know where this place was.

The puzzle lay on the ground in all its flawed realized glory. The spotted marble floor peeked through the bits where the pieces were missing. I looked at the picture and, for the first time, saw the jagged lines running across the picture and how the cut of the puzzle distorted parts of the picture, making bits of the image seem warped instead of a pristine, flat image. Somehow, the jagged lines contorting the picture troubled and saddened me much more than the many missing pieces of the puzzle. The missing pieces did not take away anything from the final picture, but those lines that I noticed for the first time ever did. But that minuscule deformity running through the whole picture is the nature of jigsaw puzzles. And we are trained to ignore it, or view it as such.

I picked up the jigsaw puzzle by its ends and let it crumble apart, let gravity pull the tenuously fitted pieces apart. What pieces clung together, I crumpled in my hands, and I scooped all the bits back into the Tupperware container. I closed the lid, and digging into the back of the toy cupboard, I returned the tub into the old, dark place where such ghosts dwell, perfumed by the scent of soap long washed away.

part one
The Burden of Ashes

Hid and Found

Ask any good Chinese family. The pecking order of desirable professions is: Doctor (neurosurgeon or cardiac surgeon is best; failing a career in medicine, dentistry is an acceptable runner-up). Lawyer. Engineer. More liberal families would probably accept Accountant, and possibly an MBA from an American Ivy League university. If you are artistic, you are expected to be an architect.

These professions confer upon the practitioner's parents bragging rights of the highest order, and these rights are used to great effect in smiting down kith and kin. A well-timed brag in the battlegrounds of golf courses and aquarobics can transform others into bitter green-eyed monsters and substantially elevate one's standing in society.

Writing is just not done. Sure, it is done, but by the children of poor, sad parents who have to forgo all their bragging rights, sitting tight-lipped at family dinners and

(Horrors!) class reunions, where they have to endure scads of pity and scorn. If any writing is ever done, it is done For Fun, and possibly to win essay contests so that, again, the parents can rub it into the faces of relatives who have lesser idiot children.

This was Singapore in the '80s. Enough time had passed since the country had gained its independence— first from British colonial rule then the Japanese occupation and then from the collective peninsula of Malaya— for the children born of parents from the riotous days of the shaky, race-conscious '60s to be making their mark on the Great Society. Their parents had given them an independent country-state, and now it was time for them to make good on those droning When We Were Your Age lectures their parents launched into at every opportunity.

Academics were the equalizing factor among races and social classes. Do well in subjects that mattered, which were the sciences and the maths, and boyo, you were in. Everybody admired you. People saw in you hope, redemption, and Great Things. The kids, brought up in this atmosphere, were very much coconspirators in this whole scheme. Visions of mansions in the twisty-winding roads of chichi Commonwealth Avenue or bungalows in Bukit Timah hills and trendy lunches at the most prestigious country clubs danced in their eyes.

At home, we had tuition for as many subjects as were deemed needed. After school, some poor hapless graduate who could not get a real job would come to our house and give us extra lessons in math, Chinese, and the sciences. Parents bought assessment books that textbook companies churned out by the baleful. These were work-books filled with difficult math sums, baffling chemistry equations, and physics problems, all with the correct answers in the back of the book. Many of these very same questions had once appeared in state final exami-nations, so they were the real thing. Rumour had it that they might appear again in any given year. So parents, teachers, and children all furiously worked these into the fabric of their lives.

There were English assessment books, full of gram-mar exercises designed to help one learn tenses, vocabu-lary, sentence construction, punctuation, and all those idiomatic things to do with the English language. There were even English Composition books, in which the publishers would print examples of exemplary composi-tions, all written in crisp, perfectly constructed English sentences. No run-ons, no complex sentence structures, no postmodern meanderings, just perfect little clause-phrase or phrase-clause sentences, with one exclamation point thrown in somewhere to give it a spark of life. Some of my classmates at school memorized a whole bank of these compositions so they could regurgitate them at examination time, scribbling them down from memory, word for word. We were given sample answers for our English literature classes so we could give correct answers to Shakespeare, Achebe, and *The Crucible*. There was a correct way to write, to think creatively, and to be creative. In Secondary One, the penultimate year of our general education, when we still had art class, a classmate of mine even enrolled in art tuition, where his art tutor made him practice the same two drawings all semester so he would ace that final art exam and bring his grade points up even more.

The act of writing was not held in high esteem. It was seen as something wholly self-indulgent and a complete waste of time—time that could be better spent figuring out how to be a neurosurgeon.

In a country where the press, the theatre, the cinema, and practically all artistic expression was closely monitored by the government, writing was also an act that could conceivably get you into real trouble. It seemed like a hoary temptation to actually speak one's mind, to say something against the grain, to challenge authority.

The parents lived through the creation of the National Security Act. They witnessed Communists, Communist sympathizers, opposition party leaders, and people who were vocally critical of the government being arrested and detained without trial. The detainees had every shred of their reputation excoriated in the local government papers and were jailed for God knows how long. "Better not say anything, better not make waves," parents warned their children. "Much better you go study and become a doctor. Make loads of money. After all, in the end, it's money that talks." Writing did not promise wealth of any sort.

There were local writers and local playwrights, but they were looked on as "the artistic crowd": effeminate poofters, bored housewives, and people with real jobs who wrote as a hobby. These were people who entertained with their talent but did not contribute in any meaningful way to the Scheme of Great Things that was happening in the country.

Occasionally there would be a blip on the screen. A play would be closed down, a book banned, an occasional playwright or writer questioned by the government for certain themes in their work.

Once, a playwright was commended for his play about the plight of Filipino maids in Singapore. The play received raves in the papers when it debuted at the local arts festival. Two years later, that very same play got the poor bloke in trouble when the government found out he was acquainted with some people who may have had communist leanings. The play was held up as an example of subversive communist propaganda trying to fan the flames of class issues in the country. Much more recently, members of a local theatre company were hauled in for questioning and their company's rights to perform yanked after it was discovered that some members of the group had attended Augusta Boal's Theatre of the Oppressed Workshop in New York City. *How did the government know?* some wondered but did not ask publicly. But in the end, everyone knew that the government just knew things.

But most of the time the writers accepted their lot in this repression. They grumbled, they griped, and they dreamed of the freedoms of the West and of writing *that* scathing yet witty novel, an indictment on the government and society, which would win the Booker Prize; but then the touring company of *Cats* trundled into town, and everyone would be licking their whiskers, practicing their rendition of "Memories" at karaoke bars, and clawing for a place in the furball chorus.

Other writers simply stayed far away from the line, churning out quaint little local-flavoured comedies. True crime, detective stories, ghost stories, and romance novels were the most popular books published and read. There were a number of local novelists whose works were not terribly well read or taken seriously. Fiction and poetry and writing and novels seemed like such a Western thing, all those words and ideas. And certainly these piddly local efforts could not measure up to the canon of British literature that was the God-sent cloudstack leading us out of our native wilderness, could it now?

I enjoyed reading more than anything else. I read at a level higher than my grade, starting with Enid Blyton books and then Agatha Christie mysteries by the time I was in Primary Three. I enjoyed these fantasy worlds, these other realities, these stories.

Inspired by our reading, a friend and I excitedly tried our hand at writing our own little stories. Somehow, the other kids in the class managed to recreate these fabulous stories and get them printed in the school annual. Now, 20 years later, I suspect that their parents helped them. But then, even as I was proud of my piddly little achievements, it crushed me to realize that my 9-year-old mind could not keep up with all these other minds around me. Worse than that, my mother found the very first story that I had written tucked away in my school bag. It was a twee, plotless, illustrated-with-coloured-pencils thing: Some spaceguy gets captured by aliens, blasts them with a laser gun, and escapes. But I had trouble with the proper usage of "than" and "then." My mom was livid. Besides wasting my time on such a worthless nonacademic activity, how could I also not know such a simple thing? Severely scolded and that evening's television viewing privileges yanked, I was made to write 20 sentences, each using "then" and "than" correctly. My first stab at writing a story ended up in tears.

After that I hid my fondness for writing in my English composition classes rather than be berated and put down for my "hobby." (Yes, like stamp collecting and comic books, that was the only thing it was allowed to be. My parents tried to persuade me to switch to chess; it was a much better hobby since it used the brain, they argued.) I tore into my composition assignments like mad, writing essays and narratives. All through my school years, while my classmates hated to write these compositions once a week, I was secretly delighted to do them. It was the only thing I was good at. I had been sent to the science sequence and I was not doing too well in school. I had above-average grades, but that wasn't going to be good enough to get me into medical school, was it? Nothing but straight A's was expected.

My father was one of the first in his side of the family to go to university: medical school, and on scholarship no less. It was no small feat. My granddad, the jolly old bigamist, was a butcher (we always had the best cuts of pork). He had 12 children and two wives to support, so money was tight. Accomplishment and success were important things to the family. Dad met Mom when he was a resident working off his scholarship obligations. She was the night nurse on the ward. (I'm glad I wasn't a patient on that ward; presumably not much hospitaling was done while the night nurse and the night doctor were making goo-goo eyes at each other and plotting to go to the Rose Show on the weekend.) Mom had come to the nursing profession by defying her father—good girls from good families became teachers, not nurses swabbing at syphilitic sores and changing geriatrics' bedpans.

When your parents are both in the medical profession, everyone and the cat simply assumes that you will be too. Sitting in the back of my dad's clinic, patients often asked when my brother and I were going to take over our dad's practice—and this was when we were still in primary school. The notion of taking over the family business is a very Chinese thing. And when the family business is something as prestigious as medicine, the stakes are raised.

Among my school chums, the ones whose fathers or mothers were doctors all knew they were to follow suit. One school chum's father pulled every string, calling in favours from friends on the board of directors and the chair of the Old Boys' Association so that his daughter, who had never ever taken a science class in her school life, could rectify her shameful mistake and be enrolled in the science sequence. She flunked horribly.

In an effort to make me study more, I was forbidden to read any books that were not curriculum-related. Anytime

I was caught reading a non-textbook, I was scolded. For a few years, I even gave up reading altogether.

Then one day a few years later I discovered an old book of my late uncle's. It was *The Collected Works of Oscar Wilde*. The fat tome with its funny, sad fairy tales, weird and beautiful stories, rekindled my love for reading. I started borrowing books from the school library and the British Council library. I wandered among the bookstores looking at the books I could not afford to buy, but took note of their names so I could find them in the libraries.

I hid my reading: I read on the school bus and after everyone had gone to bed. Occasionally, my grandmother, shuffling to the toilet late at night, would stick her head into my room, catch me lying in bed with a book, and nag me for "not studying" and threaten to tell my parents.

Reading also refueled my wanting to write. So, once a week, I looked at the assignment on the blackboard and delved into that oh-so-frivolous act of writing. It could have been an argumentative essay or those assignments requiring the student to finish a narrative, given the first few lines. I wrote feverishly and happily, my pen pressed into the ruled notebook, until my fingers were cramped; it was a feeling I loved, how those digits ached and how the muscles hurt as I pulled my fingers back to crack my knuckles in order to relieve the pressure. My grades for my compositions were nothing exceptional, but in the dreary hours of school it was the most enjoyment I got from any class.

I did not think that I wanted to be a writer. I wanted

to be an actor. I had acted in a school play, a multicultural production of *The Diary of Anne Frank* in which the Franks and the Van Daams were Chinese, Muslim, and Indian, and I was hooked. I had done this without my parents' knowledge, and by the time they found out it was too late to yank me out of it. The play did well; it was one of three plays selected to be part of that year's Arts Festival Fringe.

I wanted a life in the theatre. If my parents had known, they would have been horrified. Already my mom had cautioned me about people in "the theatre." She warned me that a lot of them were "funny."

"You mean, like, comedic?" I replied, feigning innocence.

"No…homosexual!" she whispered. If only she knew. I had been having sex with men ever since I was 13 years old, and maybe all little queers find their way to the Drama Club one way or another.

I started hanging around the people in the local theatre scene. It was the first time that I socialized with other gay people. It was nice having gay friends and confidants. I had avoided the queens at school because I did not want any of the teasing and bullying they endured to be redirected toward me. Hanging out with these out theatre fags helped me overcome my own hang-ups. I started to be comfortable around even the screamingest queens.

Young pup that I was, I did not yet realize that a whole constellation of worlds has always existed within already existing worlds. But here and now I came to that epiphany. In this microworld, playwrights and writers were revered, and I wanted the kind of adoration and power they wielded. Inspired by all my readings and from watching stage productions, I thought that I too could write something fabulous, perhaps a truly subversive account of gay life in Singapore in the late '80s, which would also serve as an indictment against the government and society. I would be the toast of The Scene, profiled in the Arts Section of the *Straits Times,* where Dinesh D'Souza, the lispy, flaming theatre critic and rumoured porno maven who preferred little Noorlinah Muhammad's overenunciated performance as Anne in *The Diary of Anne Frank* to my stately, multifaceted brooding Peter, would be amazed by my brilliance. Wouldn't that show my folks what was what?

I withdrew money from my savings account, dashed down to the Yaohan electronics department and bought a typewriter (which I still have to this day), and took my first shaky baby steps toward writing. I was a Day-Glo existentialist (hey, it was the '80s), writing purple prose and utterly overblown pretentious poetry about death, ennui, and the ickiness of Life: *The seed of Eve spat from my mouth / lies barren in the futile soil!* Fueled by pop music, I descended further into the ungodly realm of Hallmark schmaltz. I was fast headed for the saccharine swampland ruled by Susan Poliz Schultz.

After royally fucking up my A-level examinations, I came to the United States to take another stab at an education. Here I quickly learned that I was bad actor. More horrifying, I was a bad ethnic actor. I had this strange accent, I was completely untrained, and I was completely uncomfortable in my body. I realized quickly that I was never any good and that my landing the role in that school production had less to do with talent than with the limited number of boys who joined the Drama Club and weren't screaming flaming queens who wanted to wear wigs, dresses, and ply on the Max Factor. I also knew that I would not get any good, no matter how much I tried. It was just not in me, and besides I could not bring myself to take acting classes. Yikes, that would be frivolous! Self-indulgent! A waste of time! Wrong! My socialization had run deep grooves into me.

In my first semester at an American college, I felt I had to pick a major and so I chose journalism. It seemed like a practical choice and it combined the best of both worlds: what I enjoyed doing and the prospects of getting a Real Job.

At Hawaii Pacific College, where they accepted anyone with a pulse, I enrolled in my first-year English class. One of the assignments was to do some creative work. The lecturer held up my work to the class as an example of "powerful" and "emotional" writing. In actuality, it was just plain bad; it was the poetic equivalent of the power ballad—all syrup, manipulation, and easy payback. Ms. Fischel enjoyed Chippendales, Michael Bolton, and Kenny G: I should have known better. But I was pleased and held my head high among my classmates. After that semester, I transferred to the University of Hawaii, and in my first semester there I sorted through the schedule and signed up for a writing class. By some sheer stroke of luck, I ended up meeting Faye Kicknosway. She was a tough broad, weird in that Midwest writer sort of way and quite intense.

Sitting in her cramped, sunny little office by a book-shelf towering with little chapbooks and small press treasures, she scribbled comments and red-lined my poems. "No," she said, "this doesn't work, and this, and this. Fix it!" she exhorted. My heart felt like it had been poked with big sharp sticks and I wanted to cry. She was brutal. I pulled out the big guns, those poems from the previous semester that Ms. Fischel had loved. Faye glanced at them, looked me straight in the eye with a horrified look on her face, and said, "No, don't ever do that ever again." She was the first person to take my writing seriously enough to not humour me.

It was enough to make anyone want to throw in the pen wipes. But one day I turned in two pieces and, to my surprise, she loved them. She offered suggestions on how to edit and shape them. Her upper-level class was going to do a reading, and she invited me to read with them.

When I showed up at the dry run of the reading, I was nervous and intimidated. But it was also the turning point of my life: Little did I know, that day would be the start of my life as a writer.

At the rehearsal there were two writers who wowed me. One was a sassy local woman who wrote these poems in the voice of a *tita,* and the other was this young, well-groomed, fey Filipino guy with big, sculpted hair who wrote these hilarious poems about his mother and about cruising the men's bathrooms at Sinclair library. During the break the two of them came up to me, arm in arm, and said how much they loved my work. They were Lois-Ann Yamanaka and R. Zamora (Zack) Linmark. We talked, and Lois-Ann invited me to join their writing workshop.

Soon, every Sunday afternoon Lisa Asagi—another of Faye's students—and Zack would pick me up and we would drive to Kalihi to Lois-Ann's house. We whipped out our poems and read our work to one another, and then proceeded to workshop what we'd written. We recommended books to one another, bought books for one another, and lent one another books. We stalked Jessica Hagedorn when she came to Hawaii. Armed with the *International Directory of Small Presses and Little Magazines* and ragged copies of *Poets and Writers,* we encouraged one another to send out work to various journals and presses. We comforted and kvetched when we were rejected, rejoiced and feigned jealousy when someone was published and the others not. We all wrote very differently but we understood one another's voices and processes and aesthetics.

Lisa, Zack, and I also hung out a lot on the weekends, drinking heavily (Lisa, conveniently, worked at the Liquor Collection at Ward Warehouse) and going clubbing. Lying on the floor in Zack's Waikiki apartment, we wrote poems and stories chronicling our obsessive love interests, our screwed-up romantic and familial relationships, our mad wild lives. We were queer for Anaïs Nin (but we now know better—that she was just a slut with a diary), Lorca, García Márquez, Barthes, Genet, Winterson, Jane Bowles. We shared our writing with one another at every opportunity, we inspired and goaded one another to create new work, we supported one another unequivocally, and we developed a language of our own that allowed us to turn the stuff of our queer little lives into something real on the page.

With Lisa, Zack, Lois-Ann, and Faye, we never second-guessed that we were anything but writers. It was that tits to the wind abandon that gave me the permission to believe that it was okay to be a writer, and that I was one. That writing wasn't something frivolous and vain.

I visited San Francisco in the summer of 1990. I went to as many readings as I could. I saw Diane DiPrima, Sharon Olds, Galway Kinnell, Robert Hass, Allen Ginsberg, Judy Grahn, and a bunch of obscure poets at Small Press Traffic whose names I have forgotten. Every Thursday night I went to Cafe Babar for their open readings. The corrugated tin walls and the secondhand- smoky air reverberated with an exhilarating intensity. Poets were heckled with unrestrained candor and applauded with genuine admiration and respect. Of course, in all the weeks that I went there I never had the nerve to read my work. I returned to Hawaii in the fall filled with what I had witnessed in San Francisco. The street poetry and all its verve, the people who flocked to literary readings, the used bookstores chock-full of treasures—Small Press Traffic's shelves brimmed over with these little books, each one painstakingly put together by someone not unlike myself. It all showed me a world of possibilities that until then I never knew existed.

On Christmas Day 1990, Lisa and Zack drove me to

the airport and I boarded a plane for San Francisco. Away from the gang, doubt set in. But the seeds had been planted and they had taken root, and I was still terribly driven to write and to send my work out for publication.

I did not ever think I could be a writer. I did not think I had anything worth saying. As the youngest child in the family, my opinions were always taken lightly, ridiculed, or ignored. My parents believed in me: They believed that I could be anything they wanted me to be. I kept my writing hidden from my parents for a long time. I knew they would think it was a distraction from the highway leading to my degree and my real job. Even after graduating from college, I still could not tell them. I did not think that I could not bear their criticism and scorn, their carefully executed frowns designed to instill maximum shame. I just could not bear to have them sully this one thing of mine in any way.

R. Zamora Linmark published *Rolling the R's,* a highly acclaimed debut novel, went to Manila on a Fulbright Scholarship, and is finishing his new novel. Lois-Ann Yamanaka has published a number of books to a certain amount of acclaim and controversy, and was recently featured on the cover of *Poets and Writers* magazine. Lisa has published stories in various journals and we are all looking forward to her first novel, if she ever gets her shit together to finish it.

Borders opened a brand-spanking-new 24-hour store in the middle of Singapore's tourist district: It has a bistro and café and is so busy that the clerks can only restock the shelves from midnight to 6 A.M.

I met up with a friend of mine when I was last home. Her dad and my dad were classmates in medical school. "Tell me about your book," she said to me over coffee. "Your mom is so proud of you, and she keeps telling my mom all about what you've been up to in the States. And all the books you've done." I'm always the last to know. Then again, I wonder what she really said.

Now my mom calls occasionally and cautions me not to write anything bad about the government or anything at all about the family, especially her. She sends me little clippings from the back of magazines, of classified ads that promise thousands of dollars of prize money in their "Poetry Contests." "Why don't you try to enter, you're good at writing, you can make some money!" she cheerfully suggests. I try to explain to her that these things are often scams. But in her mind the idea of creative writing, of parlaying my ephemeral talent into cold hard cash seems like such a sure thing.

Recently the Malaysian police arrested two people for what they had written in their E-mails. In the throes of the country's failing economy, the two had dared suggest that there was a smidgen of racial tension in the land. They were charged with "gossip mongering" and were detained without trial for two years in order to "preserve national security."

In my life, writing has been and still is something that is dangerous, politically and privately. The act of writing occupies a limboland. It is necessary but feared. It is a brave, albeit foolish act. Even writing these pages fills me with a certain dread. Growing up in an atmosphere of censorship and repression, where one generation who learns to keep silent and play safe passes those fears on to the next generation and the next, takes its toll; it does what it's supposed to do. Writing is an ongoing risk. And it is a risk that I take on, maybe because I know no better way to make sense of this mud of life. Every day I have to fight my feelings that what I do is trivial, frivolous, and meaningless. And in the end, in the dustbin of my history, when all is decaying and rotted, composting to bits, whether my work survives after me, or even survives the next few years, will remain to be seen. What I know is what this work did: It gave me the courage to speak, and to find some semblance of myself worth the words. And that act has in no small way loosened the straps on that old muzzle made in the government store and sent to every home and every parent who willingly, or perhaps not so willingly, put it on themselves and their children, and their children after that.

Bridges Remain

Wave goodbye. The family car pulls down the cul-de-sac and my brother and I wave to Mom. Her silhouette in the tinted back window is a head peeking, sticking out from behind the passenger-seat headrest, a hand waving frantically. Dad waves a bit, but he's driving, hands on the wheel. We wave and wave until the car turns the corner and with a final wave the car is gone and Chepstow Close is laced with a strange silence, as if the car had driven off with all the sounds of the street—children playing, their tricycles crushing the damp leaves piled at the sides of the road, the sound of gates creaking open and closed, the gossiping neighbours, the barking dogs, the Sunday washing of cars, the street football games. I know the neighbours are watching, but we can't see them; they're all indoors, peeking out from behind their dusty curtains. My brother and I shuffle back indoors.

The silence that hangs in the street hangs in the house too, as if we had dragged it in on our slippers.

The door flings open and Mom is standing by my bed; she wakes me up and dresses me. She takes me by the hand and walks me to her and my Dad's bedroom, and opens the door roughly. Dad is lying in bed, propped up on pillows, watching television. She pushes me forward and orders, "Say goodbye to your father."

"Bye, Dad," I say obediently. I have no idea what is happening. Dad says "Humph," more a grunt than a reply. Quincy, ME is about to solve yet another crime. She closes the door and I ask where we're going. Mom says we're going to join my brother at Grandma's and we're not coming back. I panic: What about my stuffed animals? What is to become of them? Who will take care of them? Won't they miss me and get lonely? I had carefully named them all and talked to them every day; they were my best friends. "Bring them along," she says, and we load 12 stuffed toys into the back of a cab. We ride 100 miles, take two ferries, transfer to another cab, ride another 100 miles, cross through the causeway between Singapore and Malaysia in the early dark fluorescent tinge of dawn, and arrive at my grandma's in another country at 6 in the morning. I unload all my stuffed animals but one, the batik tortoise my Aunty Jeck Lan sewed for me as a final project in her home economics class, is missing.

For the next three days, there is a mad buzz around the house. Mom eventually calls Dad and he comes to pick her up, but by then I have already been enrolled in a new school and on Sunday afternoon Mom and Dad drive away, leaving me with my guardians, my cousins, my brother, and Rupert the Bear, Yong-Yong, Humpty, Big Dog, Kola Pola Nice Bear, PiPi Xiong Mao, Winnie, Yellow Shirt, Big Monster, A-Po, and Nice Face. The adults assure me that the one lost turtle—I hadn't even named him—is a small loss. After all, look at what I still have, they say.

I wasn't supposed to be here so soon. The argument between my parents pushed the timetable of my life ahead two and a half years—only then was I supposed to be sent 200 miles to Singapore to go to school. *When he's a bit older,* the adults would say, plotting my future, envisioning my brilliant future with the advantages of the superior educational system across the border. But now, in mid-semester, in my first year of schooling, I am in the small house my mother grew up in. She grew up in different houses, but it is here where I imagine her in all the stories that she tells me. This is what I see in the house: My mother is teasing her hair into a beehive. Aqua Net in one hand spraying, hairbrush in the other working a combination pat-comb-lift. We are somewhere in the '60s. Crackling black-and-white TV sets beam Americana in static-lined pictures across living rooms across the state, mixed in with local programming favourites. Elvis, in all his Pelvis and lip-curl glory, is in her head, she's part-singing, part-humming "Love Me Tender" with the wrong lyrics, looking like one of the

Vandellas, who wants to look like a Supreme, but Chinese. Elvis in her head because my grandfather burst into her room and grabbed the record off the player and tossed it out the window. "What's this Devil's music? It's not singing. It's shouting," he yells, before snatching the record player so he can relax in the living room reading his newspaper while Jim Reeves soothes with "My Hand in the Lord's."

If he were to look in the room now, he'd see her plotting with her brothers on how to convince him to allow her to go to nursing school. He ripped the first application to shreds and tossed it out of the same window Elvis went through two days ago. Nursing and Elvis, both wingless creatures flung to the ground. "Good daughters from good families become teachers." A broken record repeated out of the old man. "A nurse…what would people say?" he harrumphs, and seeks solace in Burl Ives crooning "What a Friend We Have in Jesus."

The first few years were the hardest. My guardians—my grandmother and my aunt Jessie—were already taking care of my cousins Karen and Sharon, whose father had died and whose mother, we were eventually told, had abandoned them when they were young.

We were like some motley bunch of orphans; and I always enjoyed fairy tales about children who were orphans and had cruel stepparents. These stories ended with the children blissfully happy and the cruel stepparents reformed or dead; the children either discovered that their real parents were actually alive and under some sorceress's spell, or were adopted into loving homes with pets.

To help ease my missing my mom and dad, I was given a small framed photo of them, taken by my dad's brother some years earlier in the cable cars on the way to Sentosa Island. I was in the cable car too, but in the photo all you can see is the top of my head, just a small crown of hair. For the first few weeks I clutched the photo and cried myself to sleep. I put the photo beside my pillow. Sometimes I could hear my brother, who slept in the upper bunk bed, sniffling tears too. He had a photo of the family at a holiday to Genting Highlands a few years back.

Going to Singapore used to be fun; it was a family vacation, with shopping trips to Yaohan and the Japanese bookstore in Plaza Singapura, maybe even a few dollars to spend in the amusement arcades there. But this was different. This was a different trip altogether. This time I was left here for some reason I did not fully comprehend just yet. I hadn't even grasped the concept of time: What was a week? A month? A semester?

My parents visited for a weekend every month. In the first year of their visits, the drive took more than six hours. They had to cross one river where there was no bridge. Instead, there was a rickety wooden ferry that brought the cars back and forth. Often, there was a long line of cars backed up. Previously, many years ago, to make that trip from my little hometown to the big city there would be five such rivers to cross, but the city councils and the state governments started building concrete bridges that linked them, and the ferrymen and the food vendors that lived off the maddening rivers all disappeared and went to other pastures. But this one bridge never got made; perhaps the river was too deep, or too wide. The ferry portion of the journey was the most dreaded part of the journey. After the long wait, there was always the fear that the ferry would capsize. If we were en route home for the holidays, my mother would always turn to the back seat and tell us to *pray for safety*. Other times, we waited at Chepstow Close for our parents to show up at the gate in the evening, having said our prayers for their safety.

In my childlike mind, my parents' death was the most horrific thing I could ever imagine, more than Springy the Pekinese dying, more than losing my cherished stuffed bears. Once, while waiting for my mom at the hair salon, I watched her being placed under the huge heated-air dome that crowned her curler-pinned new 'do like some science-fiction contraption.

"What's that? What are they doing?" I asked, and Mom looked up from her *Women's Weekly* magazine and said, "Oh, they're cooking me. Soon I'll be dead." I shrieked and started crying horribly, but everyone in the salon laughed and thought how cute it all was that I was so afraid of the hair-dryer going on my Mom. And now I imagined my parents in the car, sinking in the depths of the muddy river, and I was fearful, thinking of all my childish sins that God could punish me for by drowning my parents, until I saw the blue Mercedes Benz chug up the cul-de-sac.

Eventually, of course, the bridge got built, and the

drive time was significantly shortened, if not the worry: There were stories of timber lorries smashing into cars and crushing them like tin cans, cement mixers being hauled on flatbed trucks that fell off and crushed cars, cars that smashed into water buffaloes, killing all the passengers while the buffalo walked off unscathed, all sorts of horrible twisted wrecks of car accidents. The prayers for safety changed, the worries continued.

Now the ferries were no more; bank to bank, all the rivers and channels were connected. Even the Penang ferry, the historic mass of timber and steel that fueled local novelists' and filmmakers' imaginations, which for years ferried thousands of countrymen from the mainland to the island, was threatened by the majestic Penang bridge. We were told it was a long suspension bridge, just like the legendary Golden Gate Bridge. We were told wrong; it was a regular bridge, with columns plunging firmly into the unseen bed of the channel. Only the heavy toll on the bridge kept the ferries going for a few more months.

I was endlessly fascinated by bridges. It was the year-end Primary Two examinations—fail this and you're left behind for a whole year. We were given a list of 50 words to learn, of which 25 would be chosen for the spelling and dictation finals. The examination was to be carried out over the school's public address system. That way, the entire grade of 13 classes could do the examination at the same time. Instead of the naked word, the examination sheet distributed to us came in the form of sentences with an appropriate blank, and we were to fill in the blank as prompted by the voice on the loudspeaker. *Number 6. Potato. John's mother is peeling a potato, poe-tay-toe, potato in the kitchen.* It all seemed quite simple, really, and being the annoying overprepared child that I was, I managed to fill in all the blanks before the prompt. *Number 7. Magazine. Mary is reading a magazine, ma-gah-zine, magazine in her room.* Since I finished the examination early, I decided to pass the time by constructing a bridge from my desk to the neighbouring desk using my two rulers. I carefully tucked the end of one ruler under my boxy pencilcase as a foundation and stuck the other ruler under my neighbour's pencilcase. There was a small gap between the two so I stole the ruler from the boy behind me to close the gap. By this time, of course, the proctor had come to my desk and was red in the face, screaming "What do you think you're doing?!" I looked at him blankly. This was before I had any conception of what examinations really were. (That I would discover the following year, when half of the class ended up in tears and anguished weeping when they could not finish their mock listening comprehension exams.) The proctor brought his hand down in a karate chop right in the middle of my bridge, looking not unlike some space monster destroying a Toyko bridge in *Ultraman.* "If you're finished, if you think you're so smart, just sit there until everyone else is finished and don't disturb anyone." I spent the rest of the hour making a little bridge with my ruler, bridging pencil case to pencil case, pushing my eraser across their precarious bounce, though the Stadler eraser my aunt had swiped from her office desk was far too fat and it often careened off the ruler bridge, plunging into the depths of my desk—my own instant miniature river disaster. I imagined who would be in that eraser car: that fat fairy Winston Lee who sat at the front of the class, who insisted on being called Winnie and answering every question the teacher asked; or that evil girl from the Convent of the Holy Infant Jesus who sat at the back of the bus and terrorized us. The best scenario had them both as best friends on their way to extra math tuition when that horrible horrible accident happened.

I am a bad driver. I have no depth perception and cannot gauge distances very well. I am very bad at parking, though I am improving. My dad is a good driver. Lying on the backseat of the car, I watched the speedometer and the blinking lights in the dashboard reflected on the windows as he drove us home. Even through the worst rainstorms and the heaviest traffic, we knew we would be safe. Even as he overtook timber lorries and tankers filled with explosive gases. When we went to visit my paternal grandparents in Sungei Lembing, their little tin-mining hometown 50 miles away, my dad would drive us back after dinner. In the twisty winding roads, where one false turn could send the car crashing into 60-foot ravines of mud and tin-mining sludge, I slumped against the car door, listening to the tunes blaring from the car stereo: Lipps Inc.'s "Funkytown" and Donna Summer belting "Hot Stuff" and "Bad Girl"—how my brother and I laughed ourselves silly every time the disco whistles blew staccato beats on that album, it was the queerest thing we had ever heard! Both cassettes recommended by the salesgirl at Pahang Supermarket: "Good for driving, very fast music, very good," she assured. Even as the night fell, and insects flew bugspeed into the windshield and the fog rolled in, and the car reverberated with cowbells, whistles, tambourines, and synthesized disco beats, I knew I was safe.

Once, on the way back from a family vacation in Genting Highlands Resort, the brakes failed on the steep descent from the mountains and we went flying down the narrow mountain roads at breakneck speed, but Dad, in his calm fatherly way, brought the car to a noisy stop in the stench of smoking tires and screeching hand-brakes.

This was how fathers drove. In all weathers and conditions, in all adversity and through rising floodwaters, all to bring the family home safe.

Every year, we judge the severity of a monsoon by the bridges, which ones are covered, flooded over, which ones are washed out, and which are still accessible. The phone would ring and a relative would be calling to report that a certain road or a certain bridge was washed out, under X number of feet of water, and would tell us which other bridges were inaccessible and which ones were wholly swept away, leaving a gashing chasm in the road, a death trap for unsuspecting cars to fall into its torrential maw.

In spite of the worry about floods, I loved the monsoon. I thought it was beautiful how the rain beat down in the heaviest downpour for days, crashing on the awning outside my bedroom window. I loved the deafening sound of the heavy drops smashing against the tin awning, creating such a percussive racket no one could hear anyone talk. I loved the fearsome crack of thunder and lightning and how the flash of electric in the sky could light up the whole dark night so supremely.

We looked to see how much water was rushing in the drains around the house and around the housing estate to gauge how full the storm drains were and whether the river was at a high tide, which promised a flooding for sure, or at the reprieve of low tide. By this time, the gardens around the estate were all waterlogged, prized flowerbeds ruined, blades of grass sticking out like paddy. House dogs searched for any dry spot to curl and sleep.

In the house, the marker of whether to worry about flooding was the drainage hole in the kitchen floor. If water started to come out of the hole, the situation looked grim. The water level in the toilet bowls would rise. Then bricks were brought in, the refrigerator and washing machine had to be lifted and the bricks placed under them to raise them above any flood line. The gas tanks on the stove were disconnected and put on the tables. Dinner would be Heinz baked beans on white bread, or sardine sandwiches. The lower cabinets in the kitchen were emptied, and then we'd wait. Most times, the rain eased up and the waters subsided, but on a few occasions we actually flooded.

My first flood was in kindergarten days. Furniture was moved, and we stayed on the second level of the house. It was very Swiss Family Robinson, I thought. Fishes, shoals of gray guppies, not the sort you'd want to catch and keep, not when you could get the beautiful multicoloured ones at the fish shop for a dollar, and a small catfish, whiskers and all, swam into the dining room. Always after the floods there was a massive clean-up. Mud and sludge from the drains, swamps, and rivers stained unmercifully, and the inches-thick layer was a challenge to scrape off and wash out.

Even as we were waiting for the floodwaters to subside, Mom reassured us that it wouldn't be so bad, that it was all right—after all, she reminded us, God had made a covenant with Noah that he would never kill the world by flooding anymore; the next time, it would be fire.

But it's not always monsoon. Sometimes it's so hot and dry that the tarmac steams and you see mirages, shimmering pools of water, little oases in the middle of the road.

We drive on the road leading under the new bridge to view the changing, unfamiliar river, the same one that has been meandering there all our lives. Now you can see the kampongs and ramshackle shacks, the poor fisherfolk, the stuff picturesque tourist postcards are made of; but postcards don't show the pollution, the poverty, and the scabby children playing in the diesel sludge of the river: *Wish You Were Here.*

We stop under the bridge and get out to look. My dad says that somewhere he owns a small fishing sampan; Mom says it's probably sunken already.

We look back at our small town, not so small anymore. Across the way, a dilapidated ferry is slowly making its way across the river; a lone man and his companion are sitting in the sputtering grumble of its engine, grinding its way across the fluid expanse where once, many years ago, on a bridge, upstream, I fished for stingrays that lurked on the murky floor where the salty ocean clashes with the calm city mud.

The Beginning of My Worthlessness

My guardian, Aunt Jessie—or "Jamesy," as we called her—was the self-appointed disciplinary mistress of Sunday school, the one to whom errant children were sent to be punished for misbehaving in the house of the Lord. Just the mere mention of her name was enough to send some of the younger children into tears. She was a confirmed spinster; the only man I ever remember her dating was Stephan, a dull idiot with a Beatles moptop and Engelbert Humperdinck sideburns, who came to pick her up on his scooter and take her to choir practice every Wednesday evening. But soon he faded into the woodwork and Jamesy filled her evenings first with decoupage, then with cake making.

We were living in the post-macramé age, and decoupage was the in thing. Every night, she would select pictures with inspirational verses that she clipped out of *Moody Christian Monthly* and glue them to pieces of plywood. The wood was painted black, and the plaques were then varnished, the edges filed into patterns, and a small hook jammed on the top of the picture.

The decoupages didn't sell too well at church fundraisers, so she tried her hand at cake making, learning how from a class at the local community center. Jamesy's cakes were a hit. She made sponge cakes topped with a ring of mice created out of tins of halved pears, maraschino cherries, peach slices, and fruit cocktail. The mice would sit on a layer of cream, tupperwares of which would take up whole shelves in the fridge. If her cakes did not rise or if they turned out wrong, she would be in a foul mood and the kids would all be on guard, waiting for a scolding for even the slightest offense, harsh words to send us to bed. I was always told she had a thyroid problem that accounted for her irritability. There was a scar across her neck, which she once showed me, where the doctors cut in to dig out the oversecreting gland.

Jamesy scared the multiplication table into me in Primary Two, months before it was even taught in school. She made me recite the times-tables from two all the way up to 12, while the bamboo cane hovered over me, ready to rain stinging blows on my arms, legs, back, and buttocks if I should falter or hesitate. I learned spelling and vocabulary, synonyms and antonyms, similes and grammar with the threat of being caned. She told everyone that I was the lazy one and I had to be pushed, watched every step of the way. Every night, she made me do my homework in the hot kitchen at the end of her cake-making table, where she kept an eye on me while sifting and mixing and separating.

Every Sunday morning, we were roused out of bed at 7 A.M. A breakfast of milk and bread or cake chugged down, we were made to go practice our music. This was Singapore in the '80s, a country racked with overanxious parents who demanded their children excel at academics and music, and we were all made to take up violin or piano. Sunday morning was the worst day of my week. Each of us would take one room, and we were expected to practice. Being the youngest, I would always end up in Jamesy's room, practicing my violin lessons while she prepared for church. Occasionally, she would look away from her makeup, hair curlers, and blow-drying to scream and scold me for my useless, worthless talent. No one cared that my brother played two scales, maybe an arpeggio, before ending up on my grandmother's bed to read the sports section of the Sunday *Straits Times*.

I was horribly tone-deaf and I could never really tell if I was playing the right notes on the violin or not. All I tried to do was put my fingers where I was told they should be and play, hoping that it was right. I was reasonably good at faking it, but once my fingering faltered. "Play properly," Jamesy snapped. I tried, but I was scared and made more mistakes. "You need to practice more," she yelled. I made another mistake, a caterwaul issuing from the bow pulled across those four strings. "That's not the right fingering," she shouted at me, crossing the room and cracking my knuckles with the edge of the metal ruler she had nicked from her office. My fingers bled and

I started crying, which made her angrier. "You just never practice, all week, what have you been doing? Did you practice?" she demanded. "Yes," I whimpered. She returned to her makeup mirror while she let me go wash the blood off my knuckles and dab some disinfectant on them; my cousin Karen had to retune my violin because Jamesy's blow had knocked it out of tune.

Saturday mornings were no better. Roused out of bed at an equally early hour, we were made to do housework. We didn't mind participating in our share of chores, and we had our fair share, all mapped out on a schedule pinned to the softboard in Jamesy's room. But Jamesy's idea of housework went beyond mere chores. Every week, Jamesy made my brother and me get down on our hands and knees and scour the driveway with coconut husk brushes and Vim. She would occasionally come by to check on us. If she saw any discoloration from the even gray she expected the driveway to be, she would scream and scold. Her greatest vexation was the stains left by the fruits and flowers of the sea almond trees that lined our cul-de-sac. The sap from the falling fruit and foliage would leave small black dots, no bigger than a fat period, on the driveway. If she saw that any of these were not properly scrubbed off, she would threaten a caning, screaming about how lazy, useless, and good-for-nothing we were. After the driveway, we were to wash and wax her car to her satisfaction.

Jamesy also had this notion that we needed to be properly nourished. Each of us had to finish what was on our plates. She hated to see "good food go to waste."

Apparently, there were all these starving belly-bloated people in India who would gladly eat our french beans, steamed okra, and liver if they had a smidgen of a chance. My brother and I had a barter system: He would eat my french beans and I would eat his beef liver. My brother also developed a system of hiding food under his plate. We sometimes piled on a huge mound of rice to hide the food we did not like to eat. It was okay to throw out plain rice, but all meat and vegetables had to be eaten.

One evening, we had boiled carrots in a horrid cabbage stew. There was something about the taste and the consistency of those boiled carrots that I just could not keep down.

"Can I not eat the carrots?" I asked hopefully.

"You better finish it," Jamesy snapped. The rest of the table was silent. My brother and cousins and grandmother ate in silence. They knew what was about to happen.

"I don't like them," I said, again hoping for some reprieve.

"Sharon, go get the cane," Jamesy ordered. My cousin Sharon hesitated. "Didn't you hear me?" Jamesy's voice became a loud screech. Sharon reluctantly went to fetch the bamboo cane.

"You better eat your carrots!" Jamesy repeated. I tried to eat them by dulling the taste with some rice and meats, but it was difficult. But with the cane hovering, I dutifully put spoonful after spoonful of boiled carrot into me. Then I did the unthinkable. I vomited. A rush of chewed-up, mucus-covered carrot mush spewed out of my mouth onto my dinner plate, trailing to the floor.

Jamesy exploded. With her left hand, she grabbed me and pulled me off my stool, and with the bamboo cane in her right hand she swatted me repeatedly. She dumped me back on the stool, then took the spoon, scooped up the spewed carrots from my plate, and held the spoon to my face. "Open your mouth," she screamed. Through my tears and heaving sobs I tried, but I just couldn't. "Open your mouth, and this time you better eat it," she scolded. She swatted at me again but missed and hit the metal legs of the stool in a loud clang.

I opened my mouth and swallowed the spoonful of slimy saliva-bubble-coated carrot mush. Jamesy then scrapped what she could off the floor and I ate that too. The rest of the table was quiet. We finished our meal in silence. So many meals were eaten in this silent hostile air, created by Jamesy's constant arguments with my grandma about money or with Karen over every aspect of her life. A mere word, a slurp, some insignificant thing would trigger more shouting, scolding, threats of canings, and even more arguing.

My cousins Sharon and Karen later told me that I had it easy. Before I came to live with Jamesy, they were forced to eat a whole can of Spam each, and then too anything vomited out was shoved back down their gullet.

Jamesy was instinctively good at violence. She'd beat us then go to her prayer meetings and Bible studies. Eventually, I realized that I was the only one getting beat. All the other children had gotten older and were spared the rod, if not the harsh tongue-lashings. The stinging swats of the cane, the belt, and the back scratcher were reserved for me until the final days of my 13th year.

At the start of every school year, I had to get a set of passport-sized photos taken. These photos were used for bus passes, library cards, report cards, health reports, and other documents. Each school year was preceded by a visit to the Cathay Studios for a new set of photos. I combed my hair, put on my school uniform, and set off to the photo studio, which was run by four old men who always seemed to be in their pajama trousers and white undershirts. The equipment in the studio was as old as the proprietors. The photographer put me on the stool and made me hold up a stick with serial numbers composed out of individual wood chips, then he puttered around to adjust the golden umbrellas that were strategically placed to reflect light. The camera itself was an old, old thing. It was huge, on a trolley, and covered with a black cloth; it was the kind you see in movies of the '30s. The old man would crawl under the cloth and try to adjust his equipment. Usually I was made to sit at a slight tilt to match the tilt in the camera. Then, with a final admonition to hold still, there was a massive supernova and the pictures for the year were taken.

All this has given me a record on myself growing older in bits, year by year in the same pose, same frame, and a similar white shirt. Not unlike the evolutionary table found in biology textbooks. I look at the photos of myself at 13 and I am amazed how very young I look. Baby fat, chubby cheeks, doeful eyes, pre-braces—that would come the next year. Sure, puberty had hit: My voice had changed, and I was finally granted divine reason to quit the Sunday School Junior Choir. Small scraps of hair had started to peek out of my pubic region and under my armpits. But in the photo, I look 10. The only giveaway is the school uniform. I'm wearing a school badge instead of a patch.

I was in Secondary One (seventh grade). It was to signify a Great Change in my life. "You will no longer be spoon-fed! You are no longer children, you are all young adults and you will conduct yourselves as such!" boomed principal Ernest Lau over the P.A. of the auditorium on Orientation Day. Secondary School was difficult: a new series of subjects, new schooling environment, new expectations. I did not feel any older or more mature even though I was constantly told I was.

One day, on the bus to shop class, this ugly fuck of a man sat in the seat behind me and put his foot in the crack of the seat. He was skinny, with a patchy, pencil-thin mustache that besotted his oily face. I ignored him for most of the trip. I did notice that he changed buses when I did, but this time he sat beside me. He tried a little small talk and then he suddenly and very nervously put his hand on my crotch. It never occurred to me to tell him not to. I'm not sure if I agreed to or not but he managed to get me to follow him to a nearby restroom at another secondary school, "to play." In the bathroom stall, lit by two scant rows of fluorescent lights, half of them burnt out or flickering, he tried to kiss me, but I was too nauseated to do that. He sucked my nipples and played with my dick. I had no idea what to do. He then

50

tried to get me to suck his dick. This, I knew, was what was expected of me, but I just could not put his ugly, foul-smelling penis into my mouth, and when he forced his dick into my mouth I gagged so hard I started vomiting. Undaunted, he tried to fuck me in the arse. Thankfully, he came prematurely. He pulled up his trousers and left me in the toilet stall, confused, frightened, crying, and praying to God for forgiveness at my horrible sin. I spent a good deal of time locked in the stall, trying to clean up, trying to wipe the smell of that act off with wet toilet paper, but it seemed that I was doused in the stench of that man and what he had done.

All this should have soured me on men's penises, but it only made me more confused and needful. One day later that year, something accidental happened that would change my life. I discovered that at a urinal I could actually see someone's penis. I was ecstatic and fearful, but I wanted more. One day, at a local shopping mall, as I was trying to sneak a peek at penises in the restrooms, a man at the urinal actually turned to me and started playing with himself. He flashed a gold-toothed smirk at me and motioned for me to come over. I was shocked and I zippered up and ran out, but the seeds had been laid. The whole world of restroom sex had opened itself up to me.

Soon I was spending a great deal of time hanging out in shopping malls and cruising the restrooms for sexual encounters. My restroom exploits started to be a great burden on my mind. The better part of the year was spent making deals with God, asking God for a sign then ignoring and rationalizing everything I perceived to be a sign, praying for forgiveness and being obsessed with raging hormones and a seemingly endless supply of dicks. I believed that it was all part of a test by God to see if I was sinning. I was.

I had known before that something was up and that I was attracted to men, but this toilet thing was a whole new realm of sin and Satan, a new level that I had never before imagined. The following months—years, to be exact—were spent praying for forgiveness and trying to purge my homosexuality through prayer and Bible study. While my classmates wondered what sex was like, content to masturbate over pinups, I was out there having my cock sucked and my arse fucked. These were grown men I was tricking with. Some were nice, and grateful for a young boy to have their way with. Some were harsh and mean. There were a few nasty encounters, brutal and painful fucks, near rapes, but through it all I never thought that I had the ability to say no. Even from that very first day on that bus.

I was scared by what I was doing, scared of God's judgment and of being caught in all those restrooms and parks, but I really did enjoy those sexual encounters. That feeling of working someone's jism out of them and having them do the same for me just felt too damn good. It was the hormones, puberty.

This is what I knew of homosexuality. That it was a sin. That gay men wanted to cut their penises off. That it would lead to a sex-change operation. That the transvestites on

Bugis Street and Rochor Canal were bad people. That the poor transvestites who could not afford the sex change and hormones had crumpled-up newspapers for tits and hung out in darkened parking lots at night, whoring. That you had to be effeminate. That it was to be made fun of. That the boys in the drama club were. That you could never have children. That in a gay couple, one would play the woman and the other the man. That it meant a life of suffering, loneliness, fear, secrecy, shame.

This was the year I realized I was helpless, different, wholly alone and defenseless. This was the beginning of my worthlessness.

During these years and more to follow, it was always pointed out to me that I wasn't good enough and that there was always someone somewhere doing better, and that no matter what I did I could still have done better.

My parents and guardians held my brother up as an example for me to emulate. He excelled in mathematics and the sciences and had no problems with his second language, even taking on a third. He got good grades and was always in the top classes at school. He competed in chess tournaments on the state level. He played football for the school. My mother bought me how-to-play-chess books for my birthday, hoping that I'd learn to use my brain. I was forced to play football with my brother and his friends. I was content to whip out the drawing block and paint, but this was frowned upon. Every time I was caught laying out newspaper for an art project, I was scolded and lectured about how I was wasting my time, better I should go and study, or play football. Reading was also frowned upon. I enjoyed having my storybooks: I loved the fantasy worlds of Enid Blyton. I moved from Nancy Drew mysteries to Agatha Christie mysteries. I thought Hercule Poirot was so cool. But these were not school-related, so more scoldings followed. And if I spent too much time on my English literature work, I was scolded for again wasting time that should have been spent on "more important subjects."

Dad was a doctor and Mom was a nurse. It was expected that my brother and I would end up in the medical profession. I faked an interest in biology and zoology. I told everyone I was going to be a veterinarian. I was always referred to as the Artistic One, but what good was that? An artistic bent should lead to a career in architecture. "You like art, why don't you consider architecture?" my mother told me repeatedly at dinner, and Dad nodded.

It wasn't just my parents and guardians, it was the whole damn nation. Everyone was defined by their academic achievements. So much emphasis was placed on education, and I was a royal fuck-up. At certain points, I'm sure my mom and dad thought that I was possibly the most worthless thing that could ever happen to them. They couldn't brag to relatives and to their friends about my grades. I was just not trying hard enough, I kept hearing. But I was trapped in classes and subjects that I didn't care about, taught by teachers who were wholly uninspired and probably stuck in the profession because they couldn't do anything else. I was always far behind in my classes; I tried to catch up but couldn't. My parents nagged, bribed, and pleaded. Later, after I had bombed on my A level examinations, my folks thought it might be better if I just went to work in my father's friend's flour mill instead of wasting money and time to go to university.

While my brother's later failures in school had to do with bad choices, girlfriend problems, and other distractions, mine had to do with myself. While my parents saw glimmers of hope radiating from my brother, they saw in me a challenge to make something of my inadequacy. My father, who was the silent sort, was seething in anger and frustration under his quiet exterior.

My brother was also constantly told that he was good-looking, and he embraced the compliment wholeheartedly. He filled photo album after photo album with snapshots of himself in various poses and outfits, while I didn't have a smudge of interest in even filling a single one. I hated to be photographed; I was terribly uncomfortable looking at myself.

By no fault of his own, my brother managed to make me feel stupid, ugly, and worthless.

In school, I was nobody. I was not smart enough to be one of the smart kids, not artsy enough to be one of the talented kids who sang and danced at the annual Drama Club productions, not rebellious enough to be one of the bad kids, not hip enough to be one of the cool kids. I was beige, a dull gray, sitting behind a desk passing each day in no exceptional way. Everyone around me seemed to be in school plays and national choirs, competing in sports competitions, going on fabulous holidays, and plotting their brilliant careers. I had friends, but for some reason my friends and I never got to those scrappy boyish adventures everyone else seemed to get up to. All I had was a secret that I dared not share with anyone. In later years, when I could fake some sense of confidence, I dove headlong with wild abandon and little aesthetic sense into the teen fashion fads of the time—breakdance outfits, Day-Glo, pseudo-Madonna circa "Like a Virgin." Oh, the horror, the horror! I'm glad so few photos exist. Still, I never felt like I made any identification with or affinity to any of the established cliques. Many at school considered me "weird" or "different" or "the punk," and nothing I did could make me feel like I belonged anywhere, except in that icky queer diorama of toilet tiles, rattling partitions, and perpetually wet floors that smelled of bleach cleansers and stale piss.

At home, the beatings and caning had stopped, only to be replaced with shouting. Loud arguments between my grandmother, my cousin Karen, and Jamesy were as common as the beetles that flew into the bug zapper. Every day there were bursts of angry words that engulfed the house and reverberated through all its rooms. Arguments that lasted for hours, sometimes carrying on for days. I secretly and greatly admired how Karen was able to hold her ground and stand up to Jamesy. I learned to be as small and as inconsequential as possible to avoid all the shouting.

I pretended to be a snail. I wanted to curl into a small ball and not move, in a place in the house where no one could see me. I dreamed of being abandoned on a deserted island, or kidnapped by the Tibetan yeti on a snow-peaked mountain. (The North American Sasquatch/Bigfoot just seemed too wet, mouldy, possibly smelly, and too much into hiking the nature trails of Northern California for the purposes of my daydreams.) I can't seem to remember much detail about that time except for an endless stream of school, homework, and not much else. It was also the last few months that we had to tolerate Jamesy. She had applied to emigrate to Australia years before and now she was actually going to go. I was so incredibly happy when Karen told me. I just could not believe that this was happening.

Life without Jamesy was so much more bearable, it seemed like an answer to my prayers. It seemed that some semblance of life had crept back into the house. My grandmother tried to maintain some of Jamesy's disciplinarianism but the most she ever got to was an annoying nagging. I stayed away from home even more, hanging out at shopping malls, the public swimming pool, or the library, pursuing the anonymous sex of my queerness with equal parts apprehension and zeal.

For a long time, I was angry with my mother because she chose to believe her sister over me, never even flinching at my tales of Jamesy's terrorizing and cruelty. "Oh, never mind, discipline is good for you. She loves you and this is just the way she shows it," Mom said. She refused to fault her sister for anything. She really did believe that Jamesy did what she did for our benefit, and that by any means necessary I would excel in academics and become a neurosurgeon. To this day, Jamesy denies ever making me eat my vomit or any of the horrors I've accused her of inflicting. When it came down to believing her sister or her son, mom chose to believe her sister. "You're too sensitive, too melodramatic," she told me. "You exaggerate." Apparently, blood is thicker than some other blood. Maybe I'm not being fair, maybe Jamesy terrorized my mom too.

But would my mother have done any different? When we were still in her charge, she was also a harsh disciplinarian, expecting my brother and me to get perfect grades in school, A-pluses, scores of 100, no less. In Primary One, I had an assignment to write certain Chinese characters a hundred times over in my square-ruled exercise book. At night, my mother would check my homework, and if she thought my penmanship was sloppy she would rip the page out and make me start over again. The only problem with this was that when she ripped the page out, the preceding page was also ripped out and I had to do that bit over as well. She would wind her Big Ben alarm clock and set it in front of me, giving me an allotted time in which to finish my writing. Inevitably, I never could, and scolding and canings would follow. And when I went to school, the teachers would question me about why my exercise book was so slim and scold me for tearing the pages out. Once, Mom picked out the English reader two grades ahead of me and decided to test my spelling. When I could not spell the words she chose, I was scolded severely and made to write those words over and over in my exercise book until

I learned. Often, my dad had to come in and intervene and tell her to let me go to sleep.

Dad was a harsh disciplinarian too, but he did not have to do much. A mere angry look from him was enough to instill a paralyzing fear. That reputation has stuck with him, and to this day many of my younger cousins are still afraid of him; when they come to pick me up to go for a movie, a car ride, or a mid-afternoon snack at the hawker centre, they hesitate to come into the house in the absence of their parents, preferring to wait in the car in the hot sun.

I clearly remember my brother, in Primary Three, sitting at his desk and crying uncontrollably. The teachers could not figure out why, and an aunt who taught in the school was brought in to talk to him. Tearfully, he revealed that he had scored 97 out of 100 on a test—the highest in the whole grade, and he was afraid of the caning he would receive from my mom when he got home.

On the very first day of his schooling life, my mom made my brother do something that I was thankfully spared from doing: She made him, in front of the entire class, present the form teacher with a bamboo cane. My brother did not want to do this at first, and my mom told him that she would wrap the cane to look like a present so no one would know. But there are few ways one can disguise a thin three-foot-long bamboo cane, specially designed for whacking errant children, bought from the sundry store at the market for 40 cents.

Another time, I refused to eat the bowl of raisins my mom had set out for me and in punishment I was made to eat a whole chili pepper, ending up in the backyard crying and trying to wash the burn out of my mouth with iced water.

Maybe it's not surprising that my mom did not believe me.

I had once written her a 12-page letter, tear-stained and bubbling with the purple prose of teenage angst, about how much I hated Jamesy, how much I hated my living situation, and the depths of misery and sadness I was in. My mom called me the day she received the letter and she said all the things she always said. The next day, she told me she had made a decision to burn the letter I had written, instead of keeping it in a big book she has, where she had diligently and lovingly collected all the letters and cards my brother and I had sent to her ever since we could sign our names.

Believe me, I said, but no one did.

My brother was pretty beefy for his age, and he was certainly the biggest and toughest among all the kids in the neighbourhood. We were, in equal parts, in awe and in fear of him; we wanted to be on his team but were afraid of crossing him. My brother, raised on a steady diet of violent Chinese kung-fu comics—which have since been banned by the government—learned how to pummel quite efficiently. My parents did not think the comics were in any way detrimental. Rather, they were pleased that his Chinese language skills were good enough to read these comics—unlike me, who had a great deal of trouble keeping up with my grade's level in Chinese. They would have been deliriously happy if I could have read even one panel of those comics without any help.

My brother used his self-taught kung-fu skills quite liberally. I was the little brother, the darn pest, and I deserved the pummeling for pissing him off in any way, whether it be touching his things, making fun of his intended girlfriends, talking back to him, or not doing as he said. He had a particular method reserved for beating me that horrified the other kids we played with and, when it was executed, made everyone nervous and want to get on his good side by cheering him on and laughing about it all.

My brother would twist my arm until I fell to the floor, where he would hold on to my arm and proceed to kick me with as much force as he could, as if he were in football practice. The impact of the side of his feet or his shoe made a vile-sounding smack when it smashed into my ribs and thighs and wherever else it fell.

Sometimes I cried, sometimes I toughed it out and adamantly refused to cry. I gave the kicking a name to dull the pain it inflicted: Japanese Massage. When he started into the kicking, the other kids would gleefully shriek, "Japanese Massage! Japanese Massage!"

Early in initial stages of the terrorizing, after one particularly painful kicking, I went crying to my mom and told her about it, but she refused to believe that my brother would do such a thing. "Did you kick him?" she asked my brother.

"No," he said. And that was that. And the kicking continued.

"Stop your crying," she scolded me. "You have to learn to be tougher. You're a boy, not a girl. No one's going to want to play with you if you keep crying all the time."

Two things here: My parents lived in mortal fear that I was too friendly with my cousin Leslie, who everyone in the family, the clan, derided for being effeminate. They were terrified of what would happen if I was to be influenced by him; how could they ever have any face in the world? And crying was one thing my dad absolutely hated. There was a certain time limit to his tolerance of our bawling, and then that was it: If we did not stop, he would "really give you something to cry about." And it did not matter what brought about the tears, whether it was falling off your bike onto the hard gravel road and tearing up chunks of flesh in your knee, or being disappointed about not being able to go to the picnic at the beach with everyone else, or just being tired and cranky. You had your minute and a half and then you had better stop.

Eventually, my mother did see my brother kicking me, and she was suitably horrified. That night, my brother and I were given a severe scolding by my dad, a frightful tongue-lashing. But we still cried for only our allotted time. My parents and my guardians believed in joint punishment. "You also…" was the commonly heard rebuke. You also are not all that saintly. You also made him do this. You also did not take care of your brother and so he did this bad thing. You also are bad. You also need to learn a lesson at the same time, now bend over.

How we disciplined in our family was a matter of

pride. The adults bragged about it at family dinners and at church. My cousins Kelvin and Sylvia endured canings on their tongue when caught telling a lie. And when these canings and the eating of vomit were brought up at dinners or social events, the adults laughed about it, proud at their child-rearing skills; and the kids were expected to laugh along, grateful that we were disciplined and not like half the brats at church.

Once, in punishment for some childish mischief, Jamesy caned me and some of the blows struck me on the face. I had horrible red welts that were unmistakably cane marks. The next day we went to church, and that was even more painful than the caning. The adults looked to my aunt, who told them I was naughty and that I squirmed when she was caning me so it was my fault. I should have stayed still to be caned, she said, and the adults all agreed. The children in Sunday school, on the other hand, just pointed and laughed and laughed like it was the funniest thing in the world.

Often, after a particularly bad caning and after Jamesy had left the house for her Bible study meeting, Shanda, the house-helper who lived with us, would take my shirt off, pull my pajama pants down, and dab calamine lotion into the welts to calm the stinging pain.

I blamed myself. I was the *hum-bau*, the crybaby, the overly sensitive one. Something was serially wrong, wholly ungrateful, and selfish about me to not appreciate my discipline. After all, didn't Jamesy teach me how to ride a bicycle one Sunday family outing at Marine Parade

Parkway? Didn't she take me to go see *Spiderman* at the Capitol after school one day? And furthermore, the other children in the family did not complain, and they certainly did not write lengthy essays about it either. Everyone else took it in stride, they forgave and forgot, they did not think it was too harsh, so why couldn't I?

We did not raise children, individuals, we raised cattle.

I have not spoken to Jamesy in years. She doesn't speak to me much after she called my mother from Perth and heard that I was gay. Recently, at my brother's wedding, I saw her again after 10 years. She is older, haggard, slower, but still as bossy and as demanding that people snap to her every whim as she had always been.

"Forgive and forget," my mother tells me.

"Don't grow into a bitter old man, forgive her," Karen tells me.

It's not that I don't forgive her, it's just that I simply do not care anymore. And besides, it's futile, pointless, utterly vain to forgive someone who feels that she has never done anything remotely wrong.

I look at her and I see an old woman who has lost her power over the children she used to terrorize—much like the wicked witch in Hansel and Gretel, if she wasn't baked but had merely grown older and more toothless and more benign. The only sad thing is that Jamesy will go to her grave never knowing how much hurt she has inflicted in her lifetime.

I keep those childhood passport photos in my desk and I still look at them from time to time and am amazed by what that young face staring back at me endured. I tell myself it wasn't all that bad and that many children all around the world have had it much worse; it's not like I was starving and chained to a sewing machine to make discount fashions, or living in a war-torn country having my limbs blasted off by land mines. Sometimes I try to think about what it would be like if it was all somehow different, but I just can't seem to come up with a vision or a fantasy that fits.

This was my life. This was how it was lived. This was how I learned better.

This is what I now know of homosexuality. That it is okay. That it is a sin if done wrong. That it is a better sin if done just right. That the boys in the Drama Club still are, and the ones that were are doing all right for themselves. That it means a life of fear, not of being found out, but of being bashed and killed. That it means a certain kind of courage, a life of struggle, of real family. That it is a part of me; that it is mine, no matter how anyone else feels about it, to use, to fall on, to bear. That it continually tests what I know of love. That it gave me shelter, even if that shelter was foul. That it gave me back some semblance of myself. And that embracing it fully brought about the end of my worthlessness.

X Marks the Spot

It is a humid Wednesday afternoon; I am walking down Shattuck Avenue, my backpack heavy on my shoulders. A homeless man approaches me. He is dressed in army surplus and looks 40-something, certainly old enough to have been in Southeast Asia fighting some mission before I was even born. He approaches me and asks if I have any spare change. I dig into my pocket, grab a small handful of coins, what change there is, and drop them into his paper cup. At that moment, his two friends, who are standing in the doorway of a deserted store, rush out with their coffee-stained paper and styrofoam cups saying "Me too, me too…" and in that very moment I am home watching kids run alongside rickshaws, alongside buses and trains scrambling for the small change that beaming European tourists throw at them. Then, at that one point of motion, one simple toss,

that one arm movement, like the flagger in a kindergarten race signaling the anticipated *Go,* the bunch of
kids get left behind as the vehicle trudges forward, accel-
erating, and the expanse between have and want, dark
and white, native and tourist, becomes as contested as
desire and object, as the kids shriek and happily dive to
the dirt ground where the spot X marks the place where
the ten-cent treasures lie, useless and pure.

Snakebite

It happened the night the python slithered into the house and draped itself on the pink and orange fake wool flowers. I thought it was some new decoration that my mother had bought. I went to touch it and it moved suddenly. But pythons don't bite, they just scare you so much you pee in your pants, then your brother tells the entire school bus about how you peed in your pants (and also how you couldn't spell *lettuce*: "Everybody eats lettuce, you eat *luttuce*.") and everybody laughs for days, which is much worse than being bitten by a python. That was the first day I never trusted my brother. Even as we shared the conspiracy of silence as we walked into the house, me with eyes red from crying out of embarrassment and he with the look of guilt. We knew that we would not say a word about what had happened because between us, we had broken two of the most sacred rules of the house: not talking about the family's business, no matter how minute or insignificant, to strangers; and not crying in front of others.

My mom kept a First Aid guidebook under the money drawer at the clinic. When I accompanied her to work, I'd sit on the chair in the back, reading the book, taking especially careful notes on the Poisonous Insects and Snakes section. How to apply a tourniquet so that when you tightened the knot an ooze of poison serum would spurt out of the puncture mark. How to heat a blade in a candle flame to sterilize it, careful not to collect too much soot on the edge. How to make an X incision. How to suck the poison out, careful not to swallow or tear the incision.

I grew up terrified of snakes. The whole idea of the slithery hissing reptile that would bite you with sharp fangs, inject poison into you, and slither away as you die was too much for me to bear.

We lived across from a marshy plot of land. There were many occasions when snakes, often inky black cobras, would slither under the crack of the door and into our house. When this happened my parents would arm themselves with bamboo canes, which were the best rod for smacking a snake dead. The cane was pliable enough so that when you brought it down on the snake, the smack and the bend would concentrate the force of the blow on the snake and not bounce back—*that* force was absorbed by your arm. Newton's law of equal opposite reaction if applied wrongly here would cost you a fangful of snake venom.

My grandmother, living on the top of a mountain in a rural area, had a vast collection of bamboo canes specially made for killing snakes. She wielded them with deft precision and could kill centipedes and scorpions with them too, smacking them with one definite and exact whack.

After a snake was killed with a bamboo cane, the cane was thrown away. It was never wiped off, washed off, and reused. The snake's head would be chopped off to ensure its total and complete death, for are snakes not the incarnation of Satan, or at the very least his demonic pets, slithering all the way from the Garden of Eden into our backyards. The snake's lifeless body was wrapped in paper and tossed in the garbage, the cane and the chopped-off head were tossed into the marsh as an ominous sign to other snakes who might dare slither into our house.

Killing a snake, a centipede, or any poisonous biting or stinging insect or reptile has always been a brave act in my family. It marked someone as able to protect the family. It was the difference between adults and children. The adults protected the children and the children were to be grateful. The concept behind it was that the adult was willing to be bit, to take the poison and the pain, to protect the child.

The first time I killed a snake was also the only time I killed a snake.

It was a group effort. We sneaked up to the snake, which was lying in the gutter. My mother delivered the first blow, which made the snake hiss loudly and convulse.

It slipped out of the gutter, but that only brought it to flat land. My arm was taut, every muscle strained, and a numbness filled my body as I brought my cane down again and again and again on the snake. The bamboo cane bounced back from the rubbery texture of the snake, and the reptile's hissing and writhing made me grit my teeth and bring the cane back to the snake's body, whacking it with a force to keep it to the ground, to stop that awful hissing and squirming.

When the snake was finally pronounced dead, my mother brought out a meat cleaver, and the snake's head was separated from its body in two hefty whacks. There are superstitions, traditional beliefs fueled by market-gossip and inherited tales, of snakes that suddenly pop back to life after surely being dead. Such was the power of evil that only a head-chopping, or burning in fire, could thwart it.

The headless snake lay on the ground; it gave a final twitch, a final spasm. The afternoon sun reflecting off its underbelly, now scarred with bruises, split into little rainbows all over its oily, translucent jet-black scales, each scale overlapping into the next, shimmering like a sequined rope. I was still shaking as I looked at the dead snake.

After the snake and canes were thrown away, I noticed that I had drawn two splinters into the palm of my hand, the results of trying to be an adult, of protecting, of using a force that I didn't know I had in me and have never ever used again.

MacNothing

The clown with the yellow overalls, red hair, painted-on red smile, and big shoes is waving to me. I want to wave back but I know he will only hurt me.

The precise time McDonald's first came to Singapore still swims in my head: 1980. And one day Mr. Ang, our form teacher, walked into class with a cardboard stack under his arm. He stood in front of the class, cleared his throat dramatically, then distributed these cards: They were McDonald's timetables with a coupon for free fries and a soft drink with an order of a Big Mac, just tear along the perforation. *Ask your mommy or daddy to read the fine print and the limitations on this deal.* Mere words, but then there was a picture of a Big Mac on the back, a line drawing in red, and there was nothing like it: two whole deckers of hamburger; such extravagance!

Things like this only happen in America.

That weekend, I asked Jamesy if I could go to the movies with my cousin, then to McDonald's afterward. She gave her permission; I called my mom and she gave me $20 spending money via my grandmother's handbag. The rest of the week was spent looking forward to that mythic double-decker hamburger.

That Saturday, after *Moonraker*, my cousin Leslie and I ran over to the restaurant. It was crowded; the line of people snaked all the way outside. I got a Big Mac, a large Coke, and large fries. (What *were* french fries? I wondered. But here they were on my tray, long thin fingers of liberally salted chips.) When I went home, I filled in my school schedule on the McDonald's timetable.

I have finally discovered the amazing thing about McDonald's. Even across 18 time zones (six if you go the other way), five states and five countries, every single burger they sell tastes similar. It's amazing how they achieve such consistency. I would think that perhaps the taste of the water, different in each country, or the type of oil would cause some variations in taste. But through Singapore, Kuala Lumpur, Bangkok, Manila, Hawaii, Los Angeles, San Francisco, Indianapolis, Washington, D.C., New Orleans, Boston, and all the small towns in between, it all tastes the same. Maybe it's just my memory, how the taste buds connect with the nose and brain to register the same taste given the same name, something Pavlovian. But I don't think so. I think it's really the same taste.

It would be strange if it were only McDonald's, but Burger King, Wendy's, and Kentucky Fried Chicken also taste like they do miles away. If anything, this lends itself to my Pavlovian taste bud theory. But either way that's the wonder of fast food: No matter where you go, no matter how foreign the counter clerks are, the food is a familiar comfort.

I hate clowns. Ever since my uncle took me to a traveling circus that came to town, I've hated clowns. They're evil and mean. My brother and I were happily watching the animals and stunts when a clown came toward us and tried to be funny. He made fun of my brother's thumb-sucking, a habit he partook of quite liberally, all day long. The clown made a silly face in front of my brother and then flicked my brother's little face towel that he carried with him when he sucked his thumb. The towel served to hide the act of thumb-sucking and to absorb the saliva that dribbled out of the corners of his mouth. The clown threw the towel on the floor in a mock clowny fit, and that was supposed to be funny too, but the dirt and sand on the floor stuck to the damp towel and my brother started to cry. I started to cry, probably because my brother was crying. The clown mimed our crying, hoping his little jests and mimes would make us happy. But we were not consoled by his horrible ridicule. Eventually, he gave up and ran off the center ring to join his clown compadres, who were trying to fit into a car that kept falling apart. All I remember now of the show is some vague tiger leaping through a fire hoop, a trapeze back flip, and that horrid clown, mocking, taunting, and spoiling a kid's first circus.

It's funny how we teach kids that clowns are friendly and that they make us laugh. Sure, they trip over themselves, smack each other in the head, and do silly things with ordinary objects all in mock fun; but normally, you would never trust anyone whose face you can't really see.

Years ago, I was told that McDonald's throws out their prepacked burgers on a regular schedule, something about keeping the food as fresh as possible for its customers. What I was told was that the bottom of the chute where the burgers slid from the kitchen to counter opened up and the burgers fell into a big bin, a pile of wasted food, thrown because they weren't fresh enough. Again, such an American conceit!

The McDonald's in France serve wine. In Germany, they serve beer. In Hawaii, they serve saimin and a really delicious Portuguese sausage and rice with scrambled egg breakfast.

In downtown Kuantan, McDonald's opens its doors. It promises to break the KFC-A&W monopoly in the town. Located in Parkson Ria, the brand-new shopping center, McDonald's in Kuantan offers, in addition to the familiar American menu of Macs and Quarters and fries, fried chicken, Ais Milo, and Air Tebu—sugar cane juice; but the smell of stale, burnt palm oil charring the soybean-all-beef-patty that clings to me when I walk by smells as familiar as the McDonald's down on 16th and Mission, 24th and Mission, Stonestown, or downtown.

In some places, you can still get your McDonald's burgers in those beautiful old retro Styrofoam containers that they used to come in. I know it's environmentally detrimental and that the containers also bleed all sorts of carcinogens into the food, but there's something so tenderly nostalgic, so uncomplicatedly lovely about those containers which existed in an innocent time, before carcinogens and global warming and melting polar ice caps and mad clowns.

The clown with the red hair, painted-on smile, yellow overalls, and big shoes is following me. He's everywhere I go. He's followed me across oceans and state lines. He's always waving at me, but I can't bear to look at him. We've been through too much together.

Smokey Robinson sings of the tears of the clown: the quintessential happy person crying the bitterest tears.

I want to see Ronald McDonald cry the bitterest tears. I want to see him break down and crumple into a sobbing heaving mess on the floor in one of his restaurants, anywhere in the world. I want to see that happy clown who promises yummy treats and pseudonutrition fall apart so bad his food will taste good again in my mouth.

What We Wish You

I always wanted a Christmas complete with snow, frosty snowmen with coal and carrot faces in the yard, a crackling fireplace, and big mugs of hot chocolate. This I got from reading children's books. Those idiotic Bobbsey Twins, that bloody Trixie Belden, and the goddamn Famous Five had the best Christmases ever: Whole books were devoted to their Christmas holidays. I still haven't gotten what I wished for. It never snows in San Francisco; the best I can hope for is freezing drizzle. The snowman I've given up on completely: On a trip to Lake Tahoe, I realized how terribly difficult it is to make one of those buggers. They're not the nice fluffy things you see in comics and cartoons or in the musical TV show *Frosty the Snowman*. The crackling fireplace, thank God, I have, though I swear I'm going to get brown lung every time I have to scoop the Duralog™ ashes out of it.

In spite of it all, I still love Christmas.

Every year, the church in Kuantan threw two Christmas parties: one for the Sunday schoolers and one for the Youth Fellowship. The sanctuary would be swept out and decorated with tinsel, the Christmas tree set up, and the pews pushed to the side to form two circular rows of seats. And then we would pray that it would not flood too badly that year.

On the designated day, the kiddies arrived. Since many of the kids came from poor families who lived in the kampungs and shophouses near the church, many were dressed in their cast-off hand-me-down Sunday bests full of lace and impossible frills and pleats, clothes which they never wore on any regular Sundays; what they wore on Sundays were their regular tatty clothes. They brought a plate, a cup, and cutlery, as instructed by their Sunday school teachers. The younger ones held on to their older siblings' hands as they walked in and sat down, doe-eyed and shy. On many, fresh from their baths for this special occasion, traces of talcum powder still ringed their necks and creases of elbows and knees.

The plates and cups and cutlery stored safely in the hymnal slot on the pews, the party would begin. Carols sung and the birth of Christ retold, the games run, the tussling for prizes, the giving of gifts, and to top it off a nice buffet and a little grab bag of sweets, biscuits, and goodies to take home.

The teenage affair was pretty similar in form, except that more attention was paid to dressing up and there were raging hormones held in check only by the baby Jesus and church decorum.

Every year, we could look forward to Eunice Fernander's cake, which she made without fail for the parties. Eunice's cake had the most evil icing on it. It was multicoloured, dusted with store-bought rainbow sprinkles, and it was thick and rich. In your mouth, you could chew it and you would feel the grind of sugar crushed under your molars, your cavities opening up and your hips and thighs getting doughier, as doughy as Miss Fernander's.

For the adults, there was the Christmas Eve cantata. Until diabetes and an amputation debilitated her, every year Mrs. Kirton played the organ accompaniment to Mr. Kirton's conducting. Mrs. Kirton played each song as if it were a slow march. A very, very slow march. After her illness, amputation of her legs (my brother and I slyly suggested buying tube socks for her for Christmas, resulting in a tight slap from Mom), and subsequent death, the Christmas cantatas become a much merrier affair, a standing-room-only gig that involved the kiddies in costumes, soaring solos, and Yin Su-Han on the organ, pounding out jazzy up-tempo tunes. She had won the national organ championships years before with her multilayered rendition of "Funkytown" and had gone on to a lucrative career as an organ instructor in the state. Parents four towns away would think nothing of driving their children hours to her home for lessons.

In our family, we would head over to the Chuas' for Christmas dinner. The Chuas knew my folks way before any of us were even conceived. The Chuas knew how to entertain, they knew how to put out a dinner table. Whereas my folks would buy loads of food from our favourite restaurants and hawker stores and put out paper plates and plastic forks, the Chuas would cook a sumptuous feast and put out real china and good silverware. Whereas my family would use old newspapers as placemats, patting ourselves on the back over how practical and money-saving we were, the Chuas had real placemats with tastefully designed motifs that suited the occasion, whatever the occasion might be. Whereas my mother would lay out islands of newspapers on the kitchen floor and demand that the youngest kids stay on their newspaper islands whilst eating their ice cream desserts so they would not drip melted ice cream on the floors or touch the walls and cabinets with their sticky fingers of sweets, the Chuas had their guests adjourn to the patio for dessert and coffee.

The Chua kids were my brother's and my oldest friends. We had played together for more than 12 years, growing up. We always looked forward to this Christmas night, the sumptuous feast and the exchange of carefully chosen gifts.

The Chuas and my folks have drifted apart since each of us kids left for college and went our separate ways. I always suspected that the Chuas thought we were boorish and uncultured, and that they were always a little queasy that we might mess up their immaculately renovated house too much.

The last time we had a Christmas together, I hadn't

been back for that holiday in six years, and I found myself back where the demons of nostalgia held me. The awkward silences, the soft scraping of silverware against fine china plates as childhood friends had nothing to say to one another, the girlfriends or absence thereof, the foreignness of a place where many happy teenage hours had been spent, the persistent croaking of toads in the monsoon dampness, gossip of the monsoon's reprieve and the threat of new floods, the pets in the yards changed and the new ones not-recognizing and cruel, the sounds of revelry from the nearby holiday resorts filtering in like distant wind chimes. And in the dark of night, the street-lamps burnt out, Christmas comes again and comes fierce as a lover's kiss.

Motherland

I have been tricked, bamboozled, if you will, conned. Hoodwinked. Deceived. Betrayed by my own mother, no less. But I only have myself to blame: I allow myself to fall into her evil snare, baited with the rosy pearls of motherly love inlaid with mother-strong guilt. And if I should resist, she will dig into her giant handbag and fish out her large-framed Photogrey™ sunglasses, the ones that turn dark by themselves, but not dark enough so that I cannot see the tiny tears forming in the corner of her eyes as she blinks and says, "Have I been a good mother?" I am rendered power-less. I have agreed to go on yet another family vacation.

Maybe this vacation won't be too bad, maybe it won't feel like a slow onslaught of the flesh-eating bacteria. And this trip is special: We're going to China. The motherland.

With the fall of communism all around the world in

the early '90s, and the need to expand trade and tourism, the Malaysian government finally lifted the travel restrictions to China for Malaysians of Chinese descent. Previously, only ethnic Malaysians were allowed to go to China, something left over from the '60s when the newly independent country was terrified of the communist influence taking over and making everyone grow cabbage for the good of the people. Only three Chinese businessmen were allowed to go to China each year to participate in the highly profitable mandarin orange trade, a big once-a-year money-maker in the January-February months leading up Chinese New Year, when the Chinese buy crates of the stuff to usher in the lunar new year with the promises of sweet citrus.

My folks are excited about going to visit the Motherland. My dad especially. This is his first visit ever and it's long overdue.

In the early '60s, in the throes of the cultural revolution, there was a lot of communist propaganda sent all across the Chinese diaspora in Southeast Asia, and my dad and his two brothers, fresh out of high school, decided that they wanted to go back to the motherland to work the land for the glory of the people. My grandfather reluctantly agreed and gave his blessings for them to go. But the truckload of pigs that was going to fund the trip overturned in the winding hills of the tin-mining town they lived in, and so the trip was canceled. Which was just as well. Otherwise, right now I'd probably be wearing fake Nike clothes, working as a tour guide, and spending my free evenings entertaining at underground open mikes in crappy teahouses all across Beijing.

My mom is preparing for the trip by having a little afternoon tea with the ladies in church who have previously gone to China. The ladies prepare Mom for all the horrors China has to offer: The squat toilets with no doors. (Advice from Mrs. Tong: You have to bring a small umbrella so you can open it in front of you to give you privacy. But remember to hold on to your umbrella at all times, because someone will try to steal it.) And the cheating merchants and the scams they will pull on you, switching merchandise behind the cash register and chucking Inferior Goods into your plastic bag. (Advice from Mrs. Tong: "You must follow your purchase every step of the way until you are in the safety of the tour bus.") The cheating merchants may also try dropping the cash you give them on the floor and stepping on it, concealing it, and then accuse you of not paying them. (Advice from Mrs. Tong: Kick them in the goolies—she did—and then threaten to drag them to the police station, where they will be sent to reeducation camps in the dried-out yak-infested provinces for 12 years.) Mrs. Tong is full of great advice. My mom takes careful notes. And the tea ends with the ladies giving my mom money and a list of things they want her to get for them, mainly quilted blankets and lace tablecloths.

The trip is a mondo family affair. My parents, my maternal grandmother, and my mom's two sisters are all coming along. My brother has escaped the horror because he is off on a cruise ship to Alaska with his new wife on their honeymoon.

I am very miffed with my mom. She concealed, for months, the fact that her older sister, my evil Aunt Jessie, was flying in from Australia to come with us. If I had known Jamesy was coming I would not have agreed to go. This horrid fact was only revealed to me when I was picked up at the airport after traveling 28 hours to get home.

Traveling with my family is always an interesting experience. Aunt Jessie will bargain with merchants to get the lowest possible price, but she does it for sport, with no intention of ever buying anything. My Aunt Anna will not stop talking about her kids, Kelvin and Sylvia, and her legion of ugly devil grandchildren and how advanced their motor skills and learning abilities are.

My two aunts have frightened my grandmother with all the horrors she might face in China. They have convinced her to forgo her sarong kebaya, the clothes she has worn for 75 years, in favour of old-lady China-style pants. "Easier to squat and pee," they reassure her.

My grandmother's legs and arthritis are acting up as well; a wheelchair has been arranged so she can be carted around. My mother is suitably guilt-ridden about her deceit regarding Jamesy, and she promises me that I will not have to do any wheelchair pushing.

The day of reckoning arrives. At the airport terminal, my two aunts grab my grandmother in her wheelchair and gleefully board the plane first, reserving as much overhead luggage space as they can.

The flight on China Southern Airlines is hell. The flight attendants are all incredibly grumpy, rude, and mean. Oh, to be a girl-child in China and banished to such a life. But it's either flight stewardess or third from the left, second tier, balancing on the bicycle with your 16 cousins at the traveling acrobatic circus.

But for the boys: Oh *bao-bei er-zhi,* precious dragon child, what depths of shame have you plummeted your family into by your choice of profession? Instead of becoming the family businessman, opening the local McDonald's franchise, engineering the Starbuck's deal, or cornering the market on Levi's 501 button-fly jeans or Silvertab 505 jeans (and to a lesser extent, the Classic 565 Stonewashed jeans), here you are, serving peanuts and trying to keep the other peasants from unbuckling their seatbelts in mid-flight.

Initially, I was excited to be on China Southern Airlines. An airline without classes. No first class, no business class, and no economy class, separated by a flimsy curtain of capitalist warfare. *Just the people's class,* I thought. Then we would watch 16-millimeter movies about corn production in the Heian province and how productivity was up 22% because of new biotech discoveries pioneered at Beijing U. But to my disappointment, the plane is divided into business class and economy. Damn you, Deng Xiaoping, and your 10-year economic reform plan of 1981.

And for the movie, we get a Chinese melodrama. It's a story about a newly married couple. After the wedding, he is sent off to battle the Japanese. (It's always the Japanese.) She bids him a tearful farewell. While he's at the battlefront, she returns to their little village to take care of their parents, and then we find out that she's pregnant. She gives birth to a son (what else?!). Her husband is elated and wants to return to be a father, but she writes to him and implores him not to return until the borders are safe. She wants him to fulfill his duties to the state. What sort of life will their child have if the borders are unsafe? She wants their son to grow up strong and healthy in a secure country. The husband complies and goes undercover in the Japanese army as a spy. He is the best spy there is: After all, he is protecting the country for his son. But then, a minor slipup, and he's captured. He's sent to a Japanese POW camp and tortured, but he refuses to give up any information. He suffers greatly but engineers a daring escape with four other prisoners. His wife, on the other hand, is working as a schoolteacher in their little village. One day she breaks up a fight in the schoolyard between the town bully and this unscrubbed runt kid. She takes the little kid under her wing and he becomes her special student. She teaches him the classics, Confucian ethics, calculus, and inspires him with a tale of a Chinese hero who captured fireflies in glass jars so he could study late at night. He grows up and she encourages him to take the ultracompetitive college entrance exams. He says it's too hard, that he hasn't got a chance, but she chastises him and reminds him of catching fireflies in glass jars. He agrees to take the exam. She gives him a flashlight, since fireflies are really hard to come by these days what with the industrial boom and dam construction cutting into the marshes. Her son, on the other hand, grows up to be a no-good-nik, a bully, then the town gangster, the layabout slacker good-for-nothing who (gasp!) steals a TV. Oh, how he breaks his mother's heart. Her student tries to talk to the son, but the son threatens to beat him up. The student passes the exams, and his teacher's joy is only heightened when, at the same time, she gets news of her husband's escape and his subsequent commendation by the general with a hero's honour. He will be returning in two weeks. She is elated, but then she suddenly collapses and we learn she has cancer. (It's a long flight.) She tries to fight it, but it is too advanced. She is dying, but she is determined to stay alive to see her husband one last time. One day, while fetching water from the well, she collapses—just as her husband is coming over the hill. He carries her to their home and they exchange vows of love. All the children whom she has taught over the years gather in the room and are sad. Her son sees the error of his ways and, in a moving monologue, tells his mother on her deathbed that it is his solemn vow that he too will be an ace student. She tells him it is not too late to do that, and they cry. Her student, in a moving monologue, tells her of how she has been like a mother to him and that he will accept the son as his brother and says that it is his solemn vow (solemn vows are big in Chinese movies) to teach and guide her son, his new brother. Her husband, in a moving monologue, tells her of his love and how he regrets not being with her all these years. And with her dying, cancer-ridden breath, in a moving monologue, our heroine tells her husband how she loved him unendingly, and of the hopes and dreams she has for her family, her students, and her country. And then, in her husband's arms, she dies. There is loud wailing and weeping. In the final scene, all the schoolchildren, her husband, son, and student stand under a blossoming tree, crying over her grave. One of the youngest children sings a song about spring and moonlight, and then the screen dissolves into a picture of a peony in full bloom.

By this time half the plane is in tears but still determined to have their half-cup of free drinks. All this almost makes me wish for a Kirstie Alley movie. Almost.

Finally, we land. I thought that my first stepping onto Chinese soil would be somewhat special. I imagined having a moment like the last chapter of *The Joy Luck Club,* where deep, meaningful things would be revealed to me as I stepped on the soil possessed with centuries of dynastic histories and my people's blood memory. But it was not to be. It was crowded, hot, humid, smoggy, polluted, and there are red guards everywhere to make sure that nobody goes amok. The lines at immigration are interminably long and there's always someone trying to cut in front of you.

Eventually, by some miracle, we're processed through immigration and customs, and the tour group gathers in the airport lobby, where all sorts of taxi touts try to get our attention. There is some confusion as to which is our tour bus and what the itinerary is. Finally, the tour guide directs us to put our bags into one van, which will take our luggage to the hotel, and we are to board a minibus to start our tour. After seven hours of flying and two hours of immigration and claiming bags, I am in no mood to be filled with awe for the motherland. But there is no rest for the wicked. No time to be wasted; it's all going to be go, go, go. We are immediately whisked away to tourist attraction number 1: Tiananmen Square.

The square is filled with tourists, kite flyers, and merchants hoping to sell you any crap souvenir for inflated prices. My Aunt Jessie gets into a fight with a kite merchant because she bargained him down and then refused to buy the kite. They're arguing loudly and she's savouring every moment of it. Maybe she'll force him to eat his vomit next.

You're not allowed to see Mao's body anymore; it's all been sealed off. Every trace of the June 4 movement a decade ago has been wiped off, and a huge clock, not unlike Macy's Millennium clock but 60 times bigger, is counting down to the date when Macao will be repossessed by China. *How our glorious motherland will be stronger and made whole again!* the banner proclaims.

We're tired, but we wander about in some sort of awe at the breadth and weight of history at our blistered, weary feet.

Our tour guide is Mr. Wilson Sun. He keeps trying to make jokes to win us over, but from the get-go the tour bus unconsciously but collectively decides that we do not like him. Most of the bus cannot understand his Mandarin because he has a very strong Beijing accent, which is quite guttural and always sounds like he's choking up phlegm. The non-Mandarin speakers resent his poor command of the English language; after all, this is supposed to be a bilingual tour, and Mr. Sun's refusal to translate effectively speaks of his disdain of overseas Chinese who do not speak Chinese.

Things are not helped when he loses half the group at Tiananmen Square. In a public square larger than Russia's Red Square, on the first two hours of the trip, eight people have gone missing. Things are really not helped when two of those people are the travel agent's aging 80-year-old parents. Apparently, there was a misunderstanding as to which corner of the square we were to reassemble at. "He never say properly!" an old lady complains, dabbing her temples with big globs of Tiger Balm.

When the group has finally been reassembled in the bus, Wilson is way pissed. He scolds the group as if we were little children. "If any of you get lost the next time, I'll leave you behind!" he threatens. Now we *really* hate him.

We're headed to an early dinner, and the tour is about 45 minutes behind because of the lost tourists. En route to the restaurant, Wilson whips out a typed A-4 paper and tries to sell us the Additional Tour Package: Panda Zoo, Counterfeit Alley, Eight Extra Temples and Other Great Interesting Sights Seen Only in China, at only a mere 200 yuan per head extra, of which he will get a commission. One of the ladies in the group attempts to bargain him down and he gets *really* pissed. Little does he know what else we have in store for him.

From Tiananmen Square, we are whisked off for a quick dinner and then to some low-grade acrobatic show. We're rushed into the show, which has already started. On the way in I cannot help but notice that across the square the cinema is screening *Titanic*—dubbed, no less. The acrobatic show is sad. The acrobats are sloppy and hardly in synch; when any of them fumbles a routine they do not do it over again, they simply scowl at the audience and carry on. These are the rejects who do not go on tour with the Beijing Acrobatic Circus to perform in front of heads of state; they probably don't even get to go to Reno or some third-rate casino in India. And after their stint here, it's P.E. teacher for them.

It's getting late but the *Cina* tourists in our group want to go buy fruits from the stalls around the theatre. Fruit-buying is a big deal. But not just any fruit, fruit grown from the sweat of the people in soil steeped in 3,000 years of dynastic history. In other words, it's all overripe and overpriced and nobody buys anything, and everyone complains incessantly en route to the hotel.

Here we have a whole busload of tourists hoping to reconnect with the motherland, but all they find are Chinese natives trying to squeeze every single yuan they can out of the overseas Chinkies. And it's amazing how Westerners came up with the stereotype of the Chinese as little, passive, demure, accommodating people. Here, everyone is oily, with big feet, and screaming at you to give them money. Think of the little old ladies in Chinatown carrying four live fowl in their shopping baskets who will swat you with a live duck to get in front of you on the perpetually rush-hour 30 Stockton bus. Now think of a whole nation of them. Think of their children.

At a little past midnight, we finally get to our hotel.

There's still the matter of sorting out room keys and we all have to be up at 6 A.M. for breakfast and the next day's itinerary. The hotel is a wee bit dodgy. I'm not sure if it's halfway being built up or halfway falling down. China really hasn't gotten the hang of this tourist industry thing. Half a century of living in communes hasn't exactly helped in kick-starting the service industry. Waiters will scold you for asking for too much coffee, bellboys will berate you for having too many bags or bags that are too heavy, front desk receptionists will grudgingly take your wake-up call and then call you a full two hours early and scold you for waking up so early.

The thing about this sort of tour group is that the tourists demand each and every meal coming to them—all three meals a day as stipulated in the tour brochure, even if that means having to wake at 5:30 to eat breakfast. The first breakfast is family-style, and the tour group is already forming into cliques who will sit together at meals and compete with other cliques to see who has gotten the best bargain shopping.

Breakfast in the belly, we're herded onto the tour bus for Day 2. Today, we're off to the Forbidden City and the Summer Palace of the Emperors. There are two additional people in the back of the bus: a photographer and a videographer. It's a cheap service, Wilson assures us, and well worth the price, so you can sight-see without the hassle of taking snapshots. At the front of the Forbidden City, Wilson attempts to get us to take a group photo (400 yuan). He tries to get the group to pose together so the photo can be taken and we can be forced to buy it later. (And if the photo *is* taken, we *will* buy it because we do not want pictures of ourselves floating about out there; it's a Chinese thing.)

The revolt begins. Group members wander off and ignore poor Wilson. He tries to get us to employ the services of the videographer (1,000 yuan), but again we ignore him. He is not going to get any commissions from anyone in this group. And besides, everyone in the tour is already well equipped with auto-focus zoom cameras and high-grade digital camcorders. Wilson is close to burning his Reeboks.

My grandma is in her wheelchair, and I am dispatched to push her around. I keep trying to get her to pop wheelies, and then we play Earthquake. Needless to say, I am not asked to push her around much for the rest of the trip.

The Forbidden City is courtyard after courtyard of stone and marble and elaborate wood-carved housing. Very much like how you see it in the movie *The Last Emperor*, which is not surprising since it was shot there. Massive, opulent, and so utterly steeped in Chinky camp. It's awe-inspiring, but somehow it also has the feel of a dead place, in spite of its history and mythology and all the tourists in it. Maybe that's what happens when something is commodified into a tourist attraction so completely.

The Summer Palace is four times as large as the Forbidden City and built on the edge of a great lake. It features a canopy-covered walkway a kilometer long, with panels each individually painted with a different decorative motif. Story: The crown prince loved his mother so much that he built the walkway so she could have shelter and a different amusing wood panel every few steps as she walked along the lake. He loved her so much that he collected all her hairs from her pillows and stuffed them into a gold Buddha. Actually, that's kind of creepy. But all the mothers on the tour group glare at their worthless unfilial children.

In the early part of the century, when the Christians came, a lot of people were taken by Western ways and started taking up Western manners and food. Only after more than a few died of digestive problems and many more choked to death on Western food did they then rebel against the Christians. If you only knew how Chinese this story is: Only by food will one be motivated to action. The emperor and empress were constantly warned about their food. Each meal had to have 135 courses, but they were only allowed to take three mouthfuls of each dish so that no one would know which was their favourite and conspire to poison them.

By lunchtime of Day 2, Wilson has conceded defeat. He failed miserably to entice any of the group to sign up for the additional tour package, our excuse being that it was too expensive. But of course the group has no qualms about shelling out cold cash for extra Peking ducks at lunch (four at our table). He bids us farewell, and as he leaves the bus a small cheer rolls off the oily headrests. A new tour guide bounds onto the bus.

Scott is young, cute, clad in head-to-toe Nike, speaks English and Mandarin fluently, is a graduate from Beijing

U., and is well-versed in history and politics. He tells us he was at Tiananmen Square during those fateful historic days, and the old ladies on the tour bus *ooh* and *aah* and want to nuzzle him into their maternal bosoms and give him a good tip for his courage and bravery. They ask for stories about the events. Was he sacred? Did many people die? What really happened? And he's only too happy to tell amusing stories and moving anecdotes in between his karaoke renditions of Babyface and REO Speedwagon songs on the bus microphone.

I tell my mom and dad that the events at Tiananmen Square, like all historic events, have a certain level of myth that is important, and that there are many different versions of what happened, even for those who were there. I argue that there were a few hundred thousand people in the square and many were simply there as gawkers, and some who weren't there are probably claiming that they were there so they can feel touched by that moment in history. But to most of the tour bus, Scott is the plucky youth with the headband and the megaphone and the plastic bag of fruits who rallied the troops. "You're just so cynical," my mom chastises. "I keep praying that God will open your heart more."

"Oh, so God is now a cardiac surgeon," I say, but she ignores my wicked cynical mouth.

"That poor boy, how he must have suffered," she tells my dad, who nods.

By the morning of the third day, the seeds of dissatisfaction have begun to sprout.

The tour group has been complaining about the hotel. Sure, it's shitty, but compared to what some of the locals have it's the fucking Hilton. Well, maybe not the Hilton, but the Motel 6. The final straw is that there were only two long distance calls allotted to the entire tour group. And a hefty deposit is required to make any additional calls. No calling cards, no credit cards allowed, just cold hard cash. People who want to call home to check on their kids are not at all happy with the situation.

Plus, the group is not too happy with the food. The food provided would be considered a feast by any regular family in China, but to the tourists it's pretty poor, especially compared to what we're used to at home. It's nothing at all like the food you get in Chinese restaurants, even the worst ones. Here the food is pretty bland, and meat is expensive, so there are a lot of vegetable dishes— potatoes, vegetable soup, ample servings of low-grade rice—and very little meat served.

Of course, having been briefed, my mother and her sisters are prepared for the bland food. In their handbags they carry bottles of achar, sambal belachan, and chili paste to spice up any meal. Each has a small bag containing packets of dried snacks and instant food in case anyone starves from the lackluster fare. And my grandmother, whose legs are in rheumatic arthritic pain, can jump out of her wheelchair, use her cane, and climb three flights of stairs to the dinner banquet hall.

En route to the Great Wall of China. Scott whips out a typed A-4 paper and tries to sell us the Additional Tour

Package: Panda Zoo, Counterfeit Alley, Eight Extra Temples and Other Great Interesting Sights, at only a mere 200 yuan per head extra. Everyone signs up immediately.

The trip is six hours on the little bus. With that much time to kill, my mind wanders into evil terrain and I have a wee realization that—and I'm probably going to be sent to some PC-liberal hell (heated by geothermal wells, where multicultural demons prong me with pitchforks made from recycled metals forged by disabled Nicaraguan Union lesbians living in a commune) for even thinking this—there's something really alluring about single white men wandering around Beijing on their own.

With my dad, I start climbing the famed stairs. The stairs are really steep and pretty high in most places, and it's a good workout, not for the faint of heart. At the third tower, my dad gives up and, bladder full, pees in the corner of the watchtower, thus sealing his bond with the motherland. I climb on to the fourth tower and would have gone further if I hadn't run out of Evian water. Again I thought, *There's something incredibly alluring, sexy even, about single white men climbing the Great Wall all by themselves, or it could just be the exhaustion playing with my feeble mind.* Going down is even harder and more of a challenge, as one's legs go wobbly from the climb up.

Most of the tour bus quit halfway to the first tower and then headed back to the square to go shopping for quilts, T-shirts proclaiming I CLIMBED THE GREAT WALL, and more fruit. Only this 72-year-old lady from the bus and I made it to the top of the mountain.

The tour is forced by the state to take us to government-approved medicine shops. The medicine shops stage fabulous demonstrations to show us how potent the pills and creams they sell are.

At the first shop we are taken to, the doctors, clad in white coats, demonstrate the power of the pills they are hawking by holding two exposed electric cords plugged into a light socket. Then the doctor's assistant takes a lightbulb and sticks it on his head, where it lights up. The crowd gasps in amazement.

The second medicine shop we are taken to is selling special creams. One of the creams purports to cure pimples, rheumatism, *and* bacterial and fungal infections. Another will stimulate the kidneys and "increase sperms and help piss remains after urination." Yet another will help those "easily annoyed with oneself."

The show here involves a cast-iron link chain lying in an open gas flame. When removed, the links glow red-hot, and the doctors in white lab coats demonstrate just how hot by placing a sheet of paper against the chain, whereupon the sheet bursts into flames. Wow. The doctor then runs his hands against the links, wincing in a great show of pain. He then shows the audience the second-degree burns on his palms. Actually, it just looks like rust from the chains rubbing off on his palms. But then, the cream, oh, the cream. With one application, his palms are as lily-white as ever.

There is a free application of mentholated snake-oil

on the necks of customers. And half the bus ends up buying ginseng, magic creams, and rhino-horn pills.

By this time, of course, I am completely exhausted from the pace of this trip. There are only so many temples and palaces that one can see before they all start to become boring slabs of old cement. Two thousand years of history and contemporary world politics would be more stimulating if I were snug in my own bed.

Inevitably, we end up at the crux of the new capitalism. The new megamall, with floor upon floor of departmental stores. I especially like the grocery supermarket. Where else can you find a whole rabbit, fur and ears and all, in the freezer? We go to the alley known as Silk Road, located beside the row of embassies and consulates. The alley consists of a multitude of stores selling counterfeit or stolen designer wear. Dolce & Gabbana, Versace, Calvin Klein, Adidas, Nike, it's all here. All you have to do is bargain like the dickens. My aunts go hog-wild with their prowess. We go to the night food market, where cheap foods and foods designed to boost one's virility, like fried scorpions, are sold on skewers and toothpicks and in greasy bowls.

At the Panda Zoo and Sanctuary, I step in panda poo. Apparently, if you're endangered you can poo anywhere you want and people will be more than elated that you're pooping in such joie de vivre. And besides, it did not look like poo at all, it looked like a pile of crushed sugar cane. Until I stepped into it, and then there was no mistaking that it was poo. But still, those cuddly, furry bears are so adorable that you've just got to forgive them and take a whole roll of snapshots of them lying on their backs in the sun eating, playing, and pooping.

Outside of Beijing, we bus to Chengde, the mountain resort playland of the emperors. The hotel in Chengde is an experience. Besides being quite filthy, with strange unknown crud wedged into the bed, in the sheets, under the beds, and in every crevice, there is only one control to all the air-conditioning units on the floor. The surly receptionist grudgingly goes from door to door to take our climate-control requests.

In Chengde, we also visit the replica of the Portola Palace, made in the middle centuries. Of course, later the Chinese decided to just invade Tibet and get the real thing. The irony of all this is lost on the tour bus's occupants, who are busy trying to get a good deal on cheap souvenirs in the provinces.

There are certain things a child should never see his father do. Unfortunately for me I had to witness my father, at the dinner table, in mixed company, do his impersonation of Babe the pig. This, of course, was inspired by a serving of fatty pork stewed in soy sauce.

Finally, home lurks on the horizon. I was filled with such joy packing for the return trip home. There is a service at the airport where they will bind your bags with strapping tape so that it looks like a poor man's sloppy Christo. This prevents any luggage handlers from cutting your bags open and stealing things. My Aunt Anna chooses to save a few bucks. Her bags are cut and rummaged through. We arrive home intact, souvenir-heavy, 12 rolls of film to be developed, and just slightly constipated from our encounter with the motherland.

So this is China. This is the land from whence my ancestors sprung. Where Westerners imagine I come from. This is the place whose ancient history, language, legends, and mythologies I was taught in school. The stage for many of the pivotal events of 20th-century politics. This is where boatloads of labourers set sail for Hawaii to work in the sugar plantations, or California to work on the railroads. This is the challenging frontier where missionaries sought to bring their religion. This is the place of invading armies, invaded territories, frightful governments, cheap labour, cheaper life, twisted foreign policies, histories and revisions, vile deaths, inscrutability, multiple beauties, misunderstanding, fetishism, and the hub of the so-much-contested existences. This is the place where a small bit of me is supposed to always wander in the air, root into the ground. Where my blood and my flesh remember their enduring incarnadine nature.

And who am I, small cricket in a big paddy field, to argue.

Underneath the clotheslines in the backyard is a small hump in the grass, a little burp in the flat backyard of sod and mango trees, nothing exceptional in that bump except that Springy the evil Pekingese lies buried there.

This is the history of soft fur at A-2316 Kingdom Park. It is a history that is documented without much fuss, not captioned in photo albums. It is a bloody, cat-scratched, dog-eat-dog history.

Dogs were the favoured pet in our town; they were protectors who barked when intruders, burglars, and strangers approached your front gate. Companionship was secondary to this practical function in a town that had an inordinate amount of crime. There were stories of some plucky dog, inevitably a Pomeranian, yapping so fiercely that the burglars abandoned their mission, dropped their crowbars and Phillips-head screwdrivers (the preferred choice for stabbing) in mid-theft. Inversely, there were stories of folks who didn't have a dog being murdered in their sleep, their drawers ransacked, the VCR and gold bars carted off through the front gate. And, more shameful, there were stories of those who *had* dogs who did not yelp or bark or growl, and their owners were stabbed to death in their sleep and had their VCRs and gold bars carted off right out of their front gates.

Sadly, all but one of our dogs would not have had the sense to save its owners. Certainly not Duke, the first one I remember, the idiot Doberman who ate his own feces, vomited it up, and ate it again in cow-like bliss until Dad smacked him with a rolled-up newspaper. And certainly not J.P., short for Jagar Pintu ("gate-watcher" or "watchman"—such a hopeful name that proved so unprophetic), the idiot German Shepherd that Dad got from a breeder. Perhaps we expected something as smart and charming as Rin Tin Tin, sleek body and handsome snout ready to lead us safely from a horrible danger like an irate snake, a mountain lion, or a gas stove explosion. Instead we got a dog whose lick was far worse than her bark.

My mom decided to offer J.P. to breeders, but the dang dog always refused to get intimate with any prospective German Shepherd studs. However one day, long after my parents had given up on trying to breed her, J.P. got knocked up by a mangy stray mutt that was so skinny it managed to walk right through the bars in the front gate. This prompted my mother to buy yards of chicken wire to wrap around the lower portions of the gate. That wrapping still stands to this day.

A litter of mangy little mixed-breed puppies, scrawny as their father, was born under the mango tree one afternoon when everybody was out. J.P couldn't have picked a worse time or place to give birth; she wasn't terribly bright, after all, that dog. The red Kerringa fire ants living in the tree swarmed down, their fat heads with cruel pincers bobbing in excitement, and started eating the afterbirth. Two of the litter were stillborn, and the mother and pups were attacked by the vicious ants. The remaining two puppies died. J.P. developed a horrid infection and was put down two days later.

Not all our dogs were of the butch variety. We had two toy dogs; you see, the best families in town were getting toy dogs, and since these little darlings had annoyingly high-pitched and equally high-decibel yaps they were not only a status symbol but also a very chic burglar alarm. It seemed the thing to do so we got Dino, the cocker spaniel that was given away after three weeks because my mom got tired of cleaning its ears, which would always flop into the dish of dog chow. Dino came with Springy, a white Pekingese. Springy and I had a lousy relationship. It barked at me viciously and I chased it around with a twig a lot. Everyone loved little excitable, shaggy Springy but me. All this was fine. Unfortunately, Springy got squished under the wheel of my uncle's 1969 Datsun.

The best dog was Bowzer, named after the lead singer of Sha Na Na. The retro-'60s lounge act, complete with greaser haircuts, had their own television variety show which was a big hit in the country. We named all the dogs that came and went during Bowzer's years after the members of Sha Na Na: Scotty (corgi, cute, big red dick which embarrassed the aunts, stupid), Jocko (mutt, stupid), Danny (mutt, stupid, gave to neighbours, bit another neighbour, dug holes in yard, ran away). One thing my parents could not stand was stupidity in their dogs.

Bowz, as we called him, lasted 11 years, and was our most intelligent dog, a great guard of his home, and a fine companion. But just as his handsome snout was beginning to get dotted with gray, the first cat showed up.

The first cat was a black-and-white-striped tabby that came around and would sleep on the wall just where the dog could see him but couldn't get to him. My mom decided to start feeding it and before long it got a name: Fieldsy, named after Garfield, who was at that particular cultural epoch a cartoon and marketing megastar. Fieldsy went from being the stray cat Mom fed to the neutered house cat that slept with anyone in the family. That darn whore cat.

Fieldsy had a great life until Samson entered the picture. Samson was a street cat. He was a tough, muscular little fucker with a split ear, his medal from many cat fights and perhaps a few dog fights too. Samson took to terrorizing Fieldsy, and somehow my mom saw fit to love both cats, dutifully separating them and giving them each their designated spaces. By this time, Bowzer was already on his way out, ignored, and the attention once lavished on him went to the two cats. When I came home for my holidays, occasions which grew less frequent, I seemed to be the only one who would sit in the garden and pet him and let him lay his old head on my lap.

After one particularly bad cat fight, Fieldsy developed horrid abscesses, and my mom decided to put him down. Samson now had full run of the house and garden, and he took to prancing around the yard, guarding his turf. His only true competitor to my mother's heart was a soft sissy cat we called Pussface. Pussface, we found out later, was really called Albert and belonged to another family who lived behind us. Apparently, Albert liked what we fed our cats (and dog) more than what he was fed at home.

My mom lavished great attention on Samson. She went to the market to buy bags of cheap fish for his dinner. After boiling the fish, she would rip out the spine (he once choked miserably on a bone, which she had to extract from his throat using a pair of forceps from the clinic) and mash the flesh with bread cubes for him, leaving the tasty head intact for him to chew on. Samson lived for many years, growing fatter and rounder and heavier. Soon, he got old and docile and forgot his street fighting ways and was mauled in a cat fight. He was sick for days and eventually Mom had to put him down too.

But just when Bowzer was poised to get all the attention again, I left home and my mom ended up adopting Ticker, my cat. I had adopted Ticker from an Australian expatriate who was leaving the country. Doping the cat with a low-dosage sleeping pill, my mom packed him in his cage and drove him the 200 miles home. He mewed miserably from his wicker basket under the seat, Mom said. The customs agents wanted to tax my dad for the cat but my dad threw a fit. "It's a common street cat!" he shouted. And luckily they relented, or the cat would probably have ended up on the street again.

Ticker had gone to ruin when I left. My grandmother, who he was left in the care of, was unable to care for him too well; my cousins simply didn't care. My brother had left for college. Ticker slowly grew thin, his fur fell out in clumps, he lived sad. When I left, there was no one to jiggle the picture frames around the house, to flush geckos out for him to catch. No one to make sure that the gecko tails were removed so that he would play with the real gecko, not their defense mechanisms. No one to rescue him when his hooked tail got stuck in the window grill. No one to rescue him when he got stuck on the neighbours' roof, which he did at least four times a week. (My rescue drill got so good I could get the ladder out, scamper onto the roof, and rescue the cat in less than three minutes.) So it was fortunate that my mom stepped in when she did.

Ticker lives the good life again. Swelled to over 20 pounds, a huge lovable thing that flops around the house, he has his own cat dish, little sleeping basket, his sarong liner, a tub of wet-wipes for his ever murky cat-arse and his ever spotting cat-twat (he is really a she), and his own indoor cat litter tray. Cat litter is a luxury; most cats are expected to crap in the clay dirt of the gardens. No other cat used litter before: Fieldsy did it under the stunted coconut tree; Samson went to the Hassan's prized rosebushes.

In the meantime, Bowzer grew older and never recovered the original clump of affection that he once had in the years before the cats showed up. Still, he was given yummy treats, tasty snacks, and scraps from the dinner table, he wasn't expected to guard anymore, and he spent most of his time sleeping and strolling the gardens, waiting for the familiar sound of the car engine so he could get up and greet Mom and Dad at the gate. Soon, he got hard of hearing, and slower too. He would not notice the car backing out of the driveway, and after getting bumped a few times had to be checked for when anyone was leaving the house, in case he was sleeping under the warm car. Soon, he spent the whole day sleeping and not eating, and Mom decided to take him on one last visit to the vet.

Ticker is the last one, Mom swears. When he dies, she has plans to reupholster the furniture, maybe buy a new rattan sofa set she has had her eye on. She wants to repaint. But until then Ticker has a place at the dinner table, where he sleeps on the seat patiently waiting for any table scrap, chicken preferably. Grandma scolds anyone who feeds him because "he'll vomit," but then she too feeds him stringy bits of peeled chicken. Grandma accompanies him when he goes out into the garden, to make sure the neighbourhood cats don't bully him. Ticker gets to hiss at other cats and Grandma will shoo them away for him.

When I go home, Ticker doesn't recognize me much. Cats are like that, I'm told, no sense of memory. He sort of remembers vaguely when I tip the picture frames for geckos, but he's too fat to do much gecko-chasing these days. He doesn't remember how I had to rescue him from the neighbour's roof almost every day until he sliced his foot up and got put into a cast. He has joint pains from that episode, *fung-sap* that acts up on cold rainy nights, his loving new guardians joke.

Two doors down, our neighbour, the wife-beating, Doberman-rearing lawyer Joseph Aw, had a little monkey, a gibbon to be exact. The little bugger was named Foo, and every morning little Foo would come over, cling to our kitchen window, and my mother would go all dewy-eyed. "He's so cute," she'd trill, and then she'd feed him nuts and an assortment of fruit. Even my stern dad thought the little bugger was cute, and smart. But apparently Foo wasn't smart enough. One day he went swinging on the electrical and telephone wires and he made a connection: positive to negative. Foo was burned to a little crispy thing. His body was stuck to the phone wire and as much as Mrs. Aw tried to knock it down, first using a long pole and eventually by throwing sneakers at it, the charred body stuck to the phone wires. So she left it. Foo hung onto those wires for months, a memorial to his loving, carefree days, until his body decomposed and fell off. His body fell off, but his arms still clung to the phone wire like notes on a score, held on by a cracking jazz musician. Eventually, those arms that would hold you around your neck decomposed and all that were left were his fingers, mere knuckles stuck to the wire.

Before my grandmother moved in with us, she raised little chicks, cute yellow fluffy things, until they were sturdy, grown hens. She'd protect them from midnight

114

strays and chicken thieves by lugging their coop into the kitchen before going to bed. And when they were full-grown and plump and in the prime of their feathered beauty and life, she'd cut their heads and legs off and cook them for dinner, innards, blood, and all served up.

A pregnant cat came into the house once and gave birth. My grandmother picked one out of the litter, took the rest of the kittens, put them in a plastic bag, double bagged it, double-tied it, and threw the bag off the town bridge. The chosen kitten was pampered, fed with fat scraps, and grew up chubby, bowlegged, and seemingly to only understand Cantonese.

We love these pets, the animals in our lives, in our own ways.

In a world of soft fur and contented purring, I never understood how my elders could be so cruel and so kind at the same time. How they could so easily drive something to slaughter, to a mercy killing, and shower love and affection on the chosen ones. How they could cook Percy the wild boar in soy sauce and ginger after letting me feed it. Something about the cycle of life, sung about in a Disney movie, something about dominance and hierarchies.

In that year when I left and my cat took my place in my mother's home and heart, all we could talk about was the cat. It was our safest topic of conversation, since the weather was unchanging and the grit of my own life was best left unspoken. The cat was showered with love and affection and protected as any child would be. But when its time comes, and it will, as it always does, the poor animal, loved as it is, will be taken to the vet and left to nap for as long as it desires, dreaming of geckos, rosebushes, tasty dinner table treats, and the soft blanket on the edge of the bed, where it could sleep all day dreaming of more geckos, more fragrant rosebushes, tastier morsels, and the humans with their unfathomable complicated love.

Tom Selleck Battles the
Manila Assembly of Lucifer

Betty, the church secretary, was possessed by the devil. This was not supposed to happen, especially not at Prinsep Street Presbyterian Church, one of Singapore's finest examples of Christian sanctity and prestige. But it did happen, and during the 10 o'clock services too, Betty's screeches drowning out Pastor Low's mumbly sermon on how to be good stewards of Christ.

Aunt Jessie, being a church deacon and a God-fearing Christian, decided that Betty should stay with us for a few weeks. Those weeks were filled with the endless struggle between the forces of good and evil, God and Satan—all in the next room. Betty spent whole days sleeping and woke periodically, screaming and speaking in tongues, which we were told was the language of the demons. The gathered elders and deacons of the church would rush into the room, lay their hands on her, and pray loudly. Some of them would speak in tongues too, which we were told was the language of the Holy Spirit. Two mystical entities having a spat through their mortal representatives in languages that sounded curiously similar; but then I was told that the devil and the Holy Spirit could simply take on the other's tongue; how else would they communicate and argue whole doctrines of theology if they didn't?

Each demonic outbreak in Betty would send my brother, my two cousins, and me dashing into my grandmother's room, where we would shut the door and peep through the keyholes, listen through the walls, or daringly crack the door open to watch heaven and earth tussle for the soul of chubby Betty. Each outbreak ended in a lull, and Betty collapsed into a whimpering mess and went back to sleep.

Every casting out of demons was crucial; it had to be done properly or the consequences would be disastrous. Every time demons are cast out of a body, the demons must find a new home: They're eager to possess. The demons like nothing better than to repossess a body, much like growing comfortable in one's apartment. And if a demon should repossess a body, it will bring with it seven more demons, each one more powerful and more evil than the first. *Hey, bring the family and your demon spawn, all of them, we'll have a barbecue beside the spleen.* In the gospels, there is a story in which Jesus cast out demons from a madman but the demons kept repossessing him, tormenting him even further. Jesus then cast the demons out and ordered them into a herd of swine; the swine, driven mad by demons, rushed into a pond, where they drowned.

Demons can be drowned, and so during each exorcism session one of the kids was sent to the kitchen to fetch a glass of water. Being the youngest, I was the one that was always pushed out of the safe room to aid in the noble task of demon-slaying, a task that I was only too glad to do. That way, I could make sure that Betty wasn't drinking from my favourite milk mug and that demons weren't lying dead in the leftover driblets of water and her spit.

Those weeks were filled with nightly prayer meetings and devotions. Even after Betty left, we continued our routine of prayer and vigil against all forms of Satan. Every night, after we kids had done our homework to my aunt's satisfaction, my grandmother would be roused from her sleep and Jamesy would lead us all in an hour-long session of hymns, Bible readings, and prayers. Our hands linked in prayer in the humid night, sweaty palms pressed into sweaty palms, we prayed for protection against the devil. We went through the house and removed anything that smacked of Satan. Wood carvings that showed gargoyle-like faces, an Air New Zealand plastic tiki keychain, the cast-iron antique metal teapot, anything that contained images of dragons and phoenixes—or looked like dragons and phoenixes, such as peacocks—were cast upon a bonfire and destroyed.

Jamesy wanted to burn the Magic Marker drawing of two cocks fighting that hung over the television, but my grandmother put her foot down. The drawing was done by her late sons, and devil or not, she would not destroy it.

The teapot was particularly difficult to destroy. The other demonic ornaments gave up their ghosts without much fuss, turning into crackling embers, their squintillion demon-red eyes piercing out of the bonfire built in the farthest corner of the back garden. The black cast-iron teapot, though, simply refused to melt, or crack, or fall apart in a way that would signify the destruction of the demons it harboured. The dragon that stretched from the handle to the spout lay in the fire, an eerie, taunting, black evil mass. Eventually, the teapot was fished out of the smoldering heap, prayed over, and turned in to the church for a proper Christian disposal. The bonfire's remains were clearly visible from my bedroom window, and the smell of the charred trinkets clung to the curtains and mosquito netting for weeks.

The furthest corner of our back garden, where the demon-killing bonfire was built, also happened to border the next-door neighbour's chicken coop, and I secretly wanted the demons to possess the Sims' chickens and two geese. How thrilling it would be to see an act of such gospel proportions replayed in the back garden.

Those days, we looked for the devil any place we could. Tapes from the United States were circulating at school in which the Rev. Jerry Anderson would preach against the satanic influences of rock music. From the rattling boombox, we listened to the Reverend Anderson's Midwestern drawl as he preached the message of Satan's all-encompassing reach and how God's love was stronger than rock music. The Reverend Anderson revealed that record companies would hold black masses to bless records before releasing them. Satanic symbols, like lightning bolts and the number of the Beast, were furtively inscribed into the albums' cover art. He would play records backward to expose the real messages hidden in them. Some bands were so satanic and so evil that they didn't even have to hide their Godless messages, the lyrics themselves were pure 100-proof evil, bands like Led Zeppelin, Styx, and the Eagles. The lyrics to "Hotel California" were deconstructed and we learned that the Hotel California was really the headquarters of the Church of Satan. Don Henley sang "We haven't have that spirit here since 1969"; 1969 was the year the Church of Satan was founded, Anderson said, and the spirit requested in the song was the Holy Spirit. He read the last lines of the song in his thunderous voice worthy of the rapture: "You can check out but you can never leave." How we shuddered.

I took some of my tapes and reversed them, and to my horror discovered satanic messages in the music of Cyndi Lauper, Michael Jackson, and Men at Work. Cute, quirky Cyndi's megaselling hit "Girls Just Want to Have Fun" was nothing more than a paean to Satan: The chugging sounds of the reversed tape very clearly had Cyndi, in her trademark squeak, repeating "Oh, Satan" over and over. "Who Can It Be Now?" Men at Work had asked in their first hit, and the answer was clearly Satan. I had to play my grandmother's *Hymns of Praise* Volumes 1 through 4 to cleanse the tape deck and to quell the heebie-jeebies I had raised. All this only proved without a doubt that the forces of evil reached further and deeper than anything I'd imagined.

In the year of my first big government exam, the

Primary School Leaving Examination that would promote me to a prestigious secondary school of my parent's choice, I was sent off to Friday night tuition. My parents had figured out that I needed all the help I could get and so I was enrolled at the local People's Action Party community centre. If we lived in the ruling party's district, why not take advantage of all the perks.

Night tuition is possibly any 12-year-old's worst torment. After class, I caught the rickety SBS Bus #103 or #136 home. The bus dropped me off at the foot of our cul-de-sac and I had to walk up the long dark lane, the street-lights almost blotted out by the thick foliage of trees lining the lane. The rustling of wet leaves and the rank smell of sea almonds rotting in the drains accompanied my fears of dark and demon. There used to be a mad dog that roamed the cul-de-sac too, but it died. Still, I knew there were legions of other rabid mad dogs waiting in line to take its terrorizing place. I said a prayer and sang hymns quietly to myself as I slowly made my way up the lane. When I could see the living-room light, I broke into a mad dash for the gate. At home, everyone else would be settling in front of the telly to watch *Magnum P.I.,* a can of fruit cocktail opened for a tasty snack. The can had been put in the freezer at dinnertime so that the contents would be suitably frosty when it was opened three hours later. The sweet slushy syrup, the chunks of squishy fruit bits, and macho Magnum solving yet another case were worlds away from the demon-encrusted cul-de-sac I had just dashed through.

One late night some years ago, my friend Lisa and I

slouched against the futon and watched a midnight movie on cable. Made in 1973, *Daughters of Satan* starred a young Tom Selleck battling the Manila Assembly of Lucifer. Tom's wife, maid, dog, psychotherapist, and his psychotherapist's most difficult patient all happened to look like the characters in a velvet painting he was coerced to buy in a ratty flea market by a mysterious old crone. The characters in the painting seemed to move about and disappear every time Tom looked at it. And he looked at it a lot. Turns out every character in the film, including the dog, was a daughter of Satan. Eventually, Tom, in all his shirtless hairy-chested splendour, was killed by the daughters of Satan.

Three hours and I never figured out why he was in Manila; he could very well have been in Fresno. Perhaps it was a favour from the U.S. government to boost the local film economy.

The Betty possession made the church aware of the power of Satan, and they decided that it was not a good idea to let the young people watch horror movies. That would be glorifying the devil, Pastor Low explained. Hence, I was not allowed to watch horror movies as a child. And so, as an adult, I went on a mission to rent all the movies that I wasn't allowed to see. *The Exorcist, The Changeling, Damien: Omen II, The Omen III: The Final Conflict, The Amityville Horror.* I rented these movies and watched them with great relish. Some of them were indeed quite frightening, and I'm glad I wasn't allowed to see them as a child. But even in the absence of the movie, the aura surrounding them was unavoidable: A sizable number of audience members watching *The Amityville Horror* each night were gripped by seizures, and ambulances were parked outside the theatre every day for the run of the movie. There were perfectly good seats in many movie theatres that were off-limits because they were haunted.

I have never seen a ghost in my life. My mother, when she was a child, lived in a big house near the beach that was haunted. Bells would chime when there were no bells in sight. At night, she would be carried out of her bed and placed beneath it, the mosquito netting still intact and in place. Her brother saw a small child ghost laughing in the corner one day. Lisa's mother bought a haunted kimono rack from the Aloha Stadium flea market.

I once dated a man who lived with a woman who was a Hawaiian priestess. She could see into another dimension and was constantly talking to spirits, he told me. She told me that once when she was in Kauai when the fog had set in and the lush island was hanging in that unmistakably scented mist, she saw the spirits coming out and lining the roads, waving to her and doing the hula in celebration of life.

The ghosts that I believed in were never so peaceful or beatific. Vengeful Chinese ghosts who burst out of hell in the seventh month to seek retribution from their descendants, malevolent Christian spirits tossed from heaven after a war lasting a millennium. Angels and demons are cut from the same cloth.

I'd like to know what it would be like to see into the other dimension, to see spirits wandering on my street among the bums and the beatniks, the skaters and the punks. In this city, haunted by loss, the streets must be overflowing with spirits in one mad endless block party. But this is not what I was taught to believe. There is a hell somewhere, and it is real. And it is possibly filled with wind chimes.

Can things change? The deserted stretch of road near our house where Japanese POW camps were set up during the occupation was said to be haunted: Hitchhikers would be seen at night, and drivers cruising at that hour would be compelled to slow down, their cars mysteriously stopping without the drivers ever touching the brakes. The hitchhikers would climb in the car, some would initiate conversation, and then they would disappear from the passenger or back seat en route. The stretch of road is now prime real estate. And Betty is a missionary. She ventures into the dark hearts of India, Thailand, and Manila to spread the word of the Lord.

Let me explain the Festival of the Hungry Ghosts. A man falls in love with a woman. She dies. He goes through much hardship to get to the seventh level of hell to find her and beg that she be released. The demon who guards that level is so moved by their love for each other that he decrees that for one month each year the gates of hell will be thrown open so the dead can visit the living.

This month is marked by the Taoists burning incense and offerings to appease their ancestors. The offerings: a sumptuous feast which the living eat for the dead, and paper-made creature comforts of houses, cars, TVs and VCRs, stereo systems, and cold cash that are burnt in old biscuit tins in elaborate ceremonies that take place on the roadside and on the pavement outside houses. What began as an act of love becomes an act of appeasement, vengeance, and fear.

Since my family were Christians, we never had to participate in such ceremonies; during this time, we were told that the devil was around in his most potent incarnations. All day, the air would be filled with incense smoke and the ash of burnt offerings. When we were out walking, my grandmother would point to the remains of these ceremonies besotting the air—with more being burnt, more being offered, more sacrificed—and she would caution me, "Be careful, don't breathe these in, hold your breath."

The Burden of Ashes

Cancerous is all I remember about the moths. Every year, around March, hundreds of moths would suddenly appear out of nowhere, somehow get through the screens—perhaps through the gaps where the elastic band holding the green netting flat against the walls was sagging—and flutter madly around the house before settling down like big black handprints on the ceiling and walls. Moth wings are nothing but millions of dusty scales held together by the finest of tendons. One swat and their insidious furry bodies become limp, scraggy legs curl, toes touch underside of abdomen, and the wings burst into ashes—a noseful as lethal as a toke of pure 10-grade 1960 asbestos.

I am thinking about moths because it is 3:30 A.M. and there is a documentary on the Discovery Channel about them and I have not seen any moths in America yet.

Where I grew up, the geckos regularly feasted on the moths that came into the house: Dark moth settles by the fluorescent lamp, thinking it is the moon, navigation. Fleshy gecko creeps out from behind the cupboard, sneaks up to moth, body bending in all stealth. Moth doesn't see gecko. Gecko darts head and tongue and grabs moth's abdomen. Moth flaps its wings violently to get free. If gecko relaxes, moth escapes but will die later, as its abdomen is all chewed up and its wings broken. If gecko keeps its hold, moth flutters until its wings crumple, disintegrate, and its body becomes a meaty morsel for gecko. Where I grew up, the geckos were the size of baby alligators.

My mother was always very scared about my brother's and my safety, that we would hurt ourselves and die. Besides the usual maternal pangs, I guess that much of her overt worry was because she got her tubes tied after I was born, in line with government policy. I was born and her tubes were tied, my dad got a tax break, and they got to choose which primary school I was to attend.

One monsoon, a family friend's nephew fell into the South China Sea during a fishing trip. A few days later his body was found, washed up, wedged between rocks, partially eaten by crabs.

Another accident that was retold repeatedly for weeks in the newspapers was of the young schoolgirl whose backpack got caught in the automatic doors of the bus, dragging her 20 feet in front of her horrified school friends before she was crushed under the bus's rear tire.

There was a rumour going around that little children, ages anywhere from 6 to 8, were being kidnapped because an overpass was being built. According to some superstition, the bridge would come crashing, foundations cracked, cement unset, if children's heads were not buried at the foot of both ends of the bridge. Whether it was true or not, it scared children and parents to death. In the evening, no child was allowed to play unaccompanied at the housing district playground; in the afternoons, none were allowed to walk home from school alone. But caution and fear did nothing and eight children disappeared before the bridge project was completed.

Every Sunday, I passed by the Methodist church where the caretaker killed her abusive alcoholic husband and cooked him into a curry and then threw him out with the trash. It was a big scandal because it was a very respectable church; even ministers of state would go there to worship.

Then there was the case of Adrian Ng, Singapore's most notorious serial killer, who lived in the Toa Payoh high-rise housing estates. He, along with his wife and mistress, killed three young girls, bled them, and dumped their bodies in the Dumpster. He kept their blood in the fridge and used it as an aphrodisiac, an elixir of youth. For weeks, the papers swirled with the tawdry details of the case, complete with mugshots and details of the threesome's kinky sex rituals. The playgrounds and marketplaces spun with rumours of witchcraft, satanism, Ouija boards, cults, and medicine men. Much of the shock expressed by the populace was how someone capable of such evil could look so ordinary and live among us, and worse than that, be getting his leg over with different women when he looked so plainly unattractive.

If I were a serial killer, I would want to seriously think about how to dispose of a dead body. One method I thought might work would be to put the body into the bathtub. Stop the tub and slit all the major arteries in the body. Drain all the blood out into the tub. Pour hydrogen peroxide or bleach into the tub until the blood becomes a colourless fluid. Drain the tub; now the body can be cut with minimal mess. Cook the pieces and throw the meal out as if it were something bad in your fridge. Dispose of the big pieces far far away from the house.

I am driving across the Golden Gate Bridge, and I wonder if there are children's heads buried at the ends.

Things you die from: Car accidents. Drowning in the sea during monsoon. Murder. Leukemia. Cancer.

Places you die: At home. In the hospital. Never in a foreign country.

How you die: In your sleep. With family. Never with "just friends."

I was watching an episode of *Family Feud*. One hundred people were asked this question: "What is the worst thing that could happen to you in a foreign country?" The contestants answered: Get raped. Get robbed. Get murdered. Get shot at. Get arrested. Get killed. All these horrors possibly occurring as a result of the number 2 most popular answer: Get lost.

The other day I was at the bus stop waiting when a man approached me and asked me where I was from. For convenience, I said Hawaii. He then asked, "How long have you been in the country?" I tried to ignore him but he insisted on telling me how horrid it was to be a Jewish bachelor during the Christmas season.

My grandma tells me that one of my uncles died after a soccer ball bashed him straight in the gut at a match. Another young aunt died as a child when the roof beam fell in and crushed her crib. Aunt Esther had stomach cancer. One of my great grand uncles had leprosy and would lose his toes and fingers when he went to the market for breakfast. I have cousins who died as babies. One of their spirits has reincarnated into a living cousin, the priest from the temple told my aunt. That accounts for her bad behaviour, he said. Another one died in her sleep. They are both buried close together in a small cemetery near the beach.

I am forgetting a lot of things lately: who's alive, who's dead, how they died, birthdays, people's names, where I met certain people, names of certain wines, passwords, pop trivia that I used to know only two years ago.

I call up my friend to ask him where a cemetery he once drove me to was. He can't remember either. Perhaps he knows but he doesn't want me to remember.

When I was younger, my dad bought *Readers' Digest* hardback anthologies for me at Christmas or birthdays.

One Christmas, I got *True Stories of Great Escapes*. In one of the stories, two teenage boys swam across the Straits of China to Macao for freedom. During the swim, one boy died of hypothermia. The other boy carried his friend's lifeless body for 16 hours in the cold choppy water until he was picked up by the Hong Kong harbour patrol. He did not want his friend's body washed back to their homeland.

I am in a foreign land that I call home. I am in a home that I call foreign. I am a tourist, visiting, browsing, taking in sights. There is something about tourists that I hate. One tour company's sightseeing tour has routed their buses past my house. After seeing the Mission Dolores, the red double-decker tour bus trundles down my street, past my big bay windows. If the weather is good, my curtains are open, and the tourists see me lying in bed at noon, still in my nightclothes, flipping the channels on the TV, cup of coffee balanced on my knee, the computer blinking in the window. Tourists believe anything they see is real, real as the place they are visiting. The vision from the tinted double-decker bus with soft reclining seats and the constant temperature inside is the truth. No denying the tenuous relationship of exhibition and reality. The display of lives and objects. The production of perception.

My parents love tours. That's the only way they will see a country. Make arrangements with a tour company and get a guided bus ride through the city, let out to touch and feel only selected things, depending on the price of the tour. The coach bus experience as time traveler, as explorer and looter, the USS Enterprise of the visitor as anthropologist—all in a language you can understand.

Bangkok: Even if it is a sweltering 90 degrees outside, the coach will be a comfy 70 degrees, and you can lean back and listen to the voice-over: *And on your left, you will see the ruins of a temple that was looted and burned many many centuries ago. We are now heading to the jewel factory where you can see how jewelry is made. You can also buy lots of beautiful, expensive jewelry at Bangkok prices....* My father bought my mother a beautiful ruby ring and a diamond ring. My mother keeps them in a Singer sewing machine gear box in her cupboard. I have never seen her wear them. In her will, the diamond ring will be left to my brother, the ruby to me.

A man I used to love died in a hospital alone. We had grown apart and lost touch. I met a common friend one day at a bar and he told me about my ex-lover. Nobody claimed the body for two weeks: His parents refused, his only sister could not be found, and the hospital was certainly not going to release the body to his AA sponsor. So after two weeks they cremated him like all the other unclaimed bodies, put his ashes into a jar, and then allowed anyone to take it. But no one did. He was buried by the municipality in an unmarked grave. I drove to the cemetery. He was buried in Lot 12, Block 86, Section D. Incredibly precise locations for a person who is nothing but ashes unclaimed.

Another memory to a fucked-up year: It is New Year's

1993, and thankfully I did not get any calendars for Christmas this year. I've run out of space on my old calendar's December, tried extending the month into the new by writing the numbers into the blank spaces after *31*, but I couldn't go very far. But what do I need to cling to the past year for? Nothing ever happened; I'm still trying to find the beauty that the damn psychic said I would find in the year gone. Nothing but these nervous days to cling to. Nothing but bones aching for some primal inspirational ritual to clean them out. What the hell else can I do?

Early European maps of China are nothing like maps of China now. Then, the maps were drawn so that the coast of China was horizontal, not the familiar vertical we know now.

In *Donald Duck and the Golden Helmet,* Donald, Huey, Dewey, and Louie are in search of Olaf the Blue's winged helmet made of solid gold, buried in a cairn of rocks somewhere in Newfoundland. They are set adrift by the crooks and navigate by stars and moonlight, much like how moths do it. They land on an apex, but the whole geography is changed, eroded by wind, waves, and rain. The bit of cross-like land marking the treasure is gone, but somehow Donald and the boys figure out the effects of the erosion, and they find the helmet as plotted out on the oily parchskin treasure map. The art of cartography places everything where it should be, until the charts are lost, the places change, or the cartographer decides that the object simply doesn't exist anymore.

I'm trying to clean out my appointment book. Put the

new fillers into the ring binder, throw out the old pages. Every year it happens: I come across the handwriting of people who have died. Phone numbers and little messages that I allowed the then-living to write in my book; and before I know it all I have left is a handwriting, the last vestige of anything really organic. Once, I crossed out a dead person's name from my address book section—one hard dark felt-pen streak slashed across *name, address, phone*—and immediately regretted it. Now I use a pencil and merely put huge brackets around the scrawled writing, two gray number 2 curves gently holding fragile information.

My favourite blanket was a quilt my mother made for me. Looking at the squares of colours and fabrics, I could match each square to a dress in her wardrobe; each square a leftover from her dressmaking. I would spread the quilt over the bed, sit and look at it until my mother burst into the room shouting "MAKE YOUR BED!"

My mother is not sentimental. I came home from school one day to find my quilt cut up into dishrags, and a new woolen blanket which worked just fine, even if it wasn't so warm. Eventually, my mother brought me a new quilt one day, bigger than the first one and thicker. This time I couldn't tell where the patches came from. None of her dresses had its colours or material. Neither did my father's clothes, or my brother's, or mine.

My mother calls me long distance. She put my old teddy bears into the washing machine today and hung them out on the clothesline to dry. She wanted to tell me how funny all my *anak* dolls looked, clutching dearly to the wire clothesline with their ears, held up by wooden pegs. Rupert was the first to need mending, so many rips that my mother sewed a pair of red trousers for him to keep his sponge stuffing in. Yong-Yong needed to get his entire head grafted back on, major surgery.

These two and my Humpty Dumpty doll my mom sewed for me are the only ones that remain. The rest were given to "less fortunate people." One evening the church pastor showed up, my grandmother let him into the house, and he carried the other bears out to his car and threw them into the boot. I cried for hours, until Aunty Jessie showed up and scolded me for not being happy with "all your blessings." A week later, the pastor's wife showed up and went through my drawers and took all the old books that my mom and dad gave me. I only wanted one back: a book of Aesop's fables that I had read and reread over and over, always remembering to skip the page with the scary picture of the big fierce lion. But that went too and I cried again and Aunty Jessie brought out the bamboo cane yelling "Stop all that crying or I'm going to whack you." She then went to the kitchen to explain to the pastor's wife over tea that I was crying because I was having a bad dream.

As much as I hate to admit it, I'm incredibly sentimental. I keep things for a very long time. Old letters, cards, silly gifts, photos, bus tickets, stubs of paper with writing on them. Once, I laid the little mementos out on the living room floor thinking it would be good to get rid of some of them, clean space for new things, make moving easier. In the end, I arranged them chronologically, watching my life start from the sofa, wind its way around the room, graze the coffee table, around the ottoman, up along the sofa again, finally touching where I first began. My cat came in and sat on a traumatic part of my life.

A friend of mine lived with AIDS for 10 years before he died. His sister told me that he died with family and friends. She had gone to Hawaii to pick him up to take him home to Minneapolis with her. But he got sick suddenly and died in the islands, where he had wanted to be buried all along. I only bring this up because I was cleaning my drawers and I found a little golden frog that he gave me when I left Hawaii. "For luck," he said. His name is still in my address book: David Grossman, framed by two delicate pencil marks holding what remains all together.

It's funny that I only remember all this now.

Years ago, my brother and I had a toy box, an old plaid schoolbag, the boxy kind that fell apart after I sat on it too often while waiting for the school bus, even after my mom kept telling me not to do it. In the bag was a huge collection of plastic zoo animals and toy soldiers. The kind you buy cheap in a big plastic pack at the market. The box contained a few different packs mixed together. There was a game my brother and I played called *ting-nung-ning-nung,* named after the approximate re-creation of firetruck and ambulance sirens. The game was influenced heavily by our weekly watching of *Emergency,* starring Randy Mantooth as the plucky paramedic who saved miscellaneous people from certain death and disaster when their cars ran off cliffs or bridges or into the swimming pool in posh Bel-Air backyards.

This was the game: We'd dump the plastic animals on the floor and pick heroes and victims. Then we'd pick a spot on the floor that was on fire, designated by a carpet design. The victims would be thrown into that spot, while the rest would be herded into the fire station, usually the sofa. Then we'd grab the animals in our small hands, yell *ting-nung-ning-nung,* and rush the firefighting plastic zoo animals to rescue the poor helpless plastic zoo animal victims.

Games these days are a little more complicated. Little Mario bonks the brick with his head, revealing a mushroom. Eat the mushroom, grow big. Bonk another brick. Eat the flower that appears. Now he has the power to spit fireballs or gets a tail to fly with. All are necessary tools to save the princess, trapped in an electronic inferno Dante never ever imagined, patrolled by killer turtles, turkeys, and other monsters.

My brother and I picked names for our little plastic animals. There was Ah-Po the hippo, and Nice Face, a kangaroo who once had a nice face until my brother chewed the kanga's face off one day. Stuck the poor animal between his molars and ground away. Later, we tried to save Nice Face's face by redrawing his features with a blue ballpoint pen. The pen smudged, and Nice Face was left with a molar-molded crater-face filled with blue ink.

At that age, evil and purity were assigned. Ah-Po, Nice Face, Big Monster, Green Monster, and the other motley bunch could either be good or bad—that was to be decided at the start of the game. Still, for every good character there was room for brainwashing, temporary insanity, and bad peer pressure, and for every bad character there was the simple act of pretending, of being a mole, an impostor, a double agent.

My mother calls me one night. She tells me she wants to have a face-lift. Why, I ask her. Children always think their mothers look good; besides, face-lifts are what the horridly vain and plump slinky wives of Chinese businessmen did, along with tattooing eyebrows and a double eyelid in a desperate attempt to recapture the fading glamour of their lounge singer–dance hostess days.

I remember reading in the newspapers about women who went to a beauty parlor to get some facial treatments or a tattoo job and the beautician botched the job. There was always before and after photos: grim proof that such awful things do happen. Once, the newspaper got the before and after photos mixed up. For a whole day, the country was torn between horror and amusement by the wrong face on the front page of *The New Straits Times*. The next day there was a small retraction and an apology in the lower left-hand corner of page 2, but by then the woman, in sheer embarrassment, had thrown herself off an apartment complex.

My mother said she would think about the face-lift.

There is a game of hopscotch that I remember very

clearly. It was in Johor, just by the Singapore-Malaysia border. My mother was not allowed to reenter Singapore, her birth country, where my brother and I were living and studying. My mom had given money to missionaries in China, and the Malaysian authorities were wary of people who had any contact with openly communist countries so they took her passport for a few months just to check on her. My dad drove across the border to fetch us. While waiting, my cousin and I played a game of hopscotch in the sandy parking lot. The game went on for at least two hours in the afternoon sun. Then my dad's car appeared. He honked his horn, we moved away, and he parked on our game board, drawn in the sand with our fingers.

The games I played as a kid had set rules. This was the boundary—this edge of the carpet, this strip on the carpet, this crack in the floor, this part of the garden marked by this rock: This is my land, my kingdom. Trespass and die. Everything was believable: See these red plastic bullets? They're poisonous. If they hit you, you will die. At mealtime: Okay, pretend you are Popeye and this is the spinach you need to get strong and then you can beat your brother up. The spoon is the rocket; the mouth is the port. The mound of rice is a desert island floating in a sea of cabbage soup; the fish balls are evil sea creatures; the cabbage, killer seaweed. In sickness: The pills are the antidote to the poison that the bad guy slipped into your body. You must take it in two minutes or you will die.

A game that I played by myself as a kid was believing that my stuffed animals would come to life at night, fueled by the Enid Blyton books I read where teddies, rag dolls, and tin soldiers moved and had great adventures after their masters and mistresses went to bed. I pretended to sleep and quickly opened my eyes to catch the slightest movement by any of my friends at the foot of the bed.

But somewhere along the way, the Enchanted Forest with the Big Tree in the middle that opened to an ever-evolving new world, pleasant, magical, or malevolent, is gone; the Magic Flying Chair is gone; the Famous Five and Secret Seven's adventures have grown stale and all too implausible. Fairies, gnomes, elves, and teddies that came to life and played and danced all night have slinked away, been killed, lost, and laid to rest.

And the space vacated by childhood games and fantasies is flooded with the inward splintering spit of adult games. Games with rules that are unspoken, implied, denser, perplexing. Games that are not as fun to play, that dig deep and brutal; perhaps not even considered games by any standard of enjoyment, but play we must, for there is much more to lose if you don't follow the rules or if you refuse to believe in the ultimate mission of it. Throw dice. Move piece. Move.

When a friend of mine was ill and dying in the hospital, he swore the figures in the postcard that I gave him came to life. I asked him to tell me what he saw. The postcard, an attempt to cheer him up, tacked to the wall closest to his bed, was of a Chagall painting: The figures flew out like angels and the room gradually turned washed-water blue, he said, all pinpointed on a scale so that each hue of blue coincided and matched with the original colour of the object or flesh in the room, just like how old movies are colourized.

Toward the end, he couldn't describe anything anymore. The language of our game went inward, and the look in his eyes replaced grammar and coherence. My friend died in a blue room with two-dimensional angels, dancing couples, frisky dogs, brides and grooms skimming the sheets, the get-well cards, the elaborately arranged flowers, the IV drips and medical paraphernalia, and his long curled eyelashes.

Man Gets Pushed Off Subway Platform, New York City

A man is pushed off the subway platform. The perpetrators run away, two red woolen caps dashing across the crush of commuters, bouncing up the stairs and gone. The man careens forward, one hand tucked firmly inside his jacket's front pocket, trapped; the other hand reaches out to grab something to hold on to. In that one pose, he looks like a *Life* magazine photograph of an Olympic runner breaking the tape in triumph. He doesn't find anything to hold on to, not quite. His outstretched hand, overhead, finds the row of fluorescent lights that line the ceiling of the station. He grabs the tube, but it doesn't hold. It snaps into two, like a candy bar, with a gorgeous sound. The air fills with electrical smoke as the gaseous insides of the tube meet the cold air. The man falls into the gutter between the tracks. The light in the station is one tube darker now, making the man's fall look more painful. The gutter between the tracks is filled with black water, the melted remains of snow and rain that sloshes through the roads, down storm drains, sluicing downstream into a stagnant river filled with candy wrappers, shreds of newspaper, potato crisp wrappers, bits of fallen clothes, take-away food cartons, empty cans of soda. The water looks like dark syrup, but when the man falls into it, proves to be thin fluid after all. A rat the size of an infant's foot scurries away; it had been standing here doing its rat things, camouflaged, all this time. The man stands up in the gutter. A woman yells, "Get out, get out, there's a train coming!" Another man shouts, "Don't touch the third rail!" The other commuters look on, horrified, waiting for that train to come. No one comes forward to help him. It is as if a giant hand is holding everyone back the requisite three feet away from the edge of the platform. The old Chinese ladies with their poultry and vegetables in their shopping baskets, the girls just out of school, the B-boys, the yuppies, the businessmen, secretaries, and office workers all look on with a calm panic, a quiet anxiety. No one says much, no one says anything at all, any noise is incidental, outside the station and from commuters who have just come onto the platform. The awful quiet is broken by the woman who again yells, "Get out, there's a train coming, get out, get out!" The man looks a bit dazed, he brushes himself off, he picks his hat out of the muck and shoves the soiled mess into his jacket pocket. The man walks slowly to the edge of the platform. He is shorter than he looked when he was falling. The edge of the platform comes up to his eyebrows. He tries to boost himself up onto the platform. Still no one comes forward to help pull him up. The woman who is screaming about the train coming is still screaming about the train coming. Finally, with a great amount of effort, the man manages to get himself boosted up, one leg on the platform, a supreme effort, and he clumsily lumbers onto the platform much like how bears climb onto crude unnatural make-believe landforms at a zoo. The commuters move away, part like the Red Sea and let the man walk away, up the stairs and out of the station. At the edge of the platform where he climbed out, there is a smudge on the tiled floor, pigment of grease and sludge from the waters of an urban Styx. Five blocks away. Or five miles. Or five minutes away, in an art gallery with walls a colour so fashionable it doesn't even have a name, a man and a woman are looking at a painting. The frame is a fat, extravagant, gilded thing with ornate petals and flowers. At the center of each side of the frame are angels' wings—no fat cherub, just wings. The canvas is a mad splatter of colour. The woman points out a path of colour for the man to follow. She holds her finger up in the air in front of the painting and traces that path. The man's eyes follow the woman's finger back and forth across the canvas but he is looking not at the painting anymore but at the woman's finger. He likes the way her finger hangs in the air as if the rest of her arm, sheathed in her green sweater-sleeve, does not exist. Across town, in an office on the third floor of an old brownstone, a young man is sitting across the desk from a doctor. The doctor holds up cards with ink blots on them and asks the young man what he sees. The man says he sees a butterfly dodging cannonballs, pussy willows having a picnic, fruitflies pretending to be the crucifixion, a small dog's cancer, a plate of tender gravied roast beef piled so high it reaches the sky and stains the clouds, the waiter from the bar he was at last night. The examination goes on and the young man is responding to the doctor's questions but he is not looking at the doctor nor the cards anymore but out the window behind the doctor. There is a pigeon with one good leg and one mangled leg with bits of wire attached to it sitting on the window sill. It is not an uncommon sight in the city. Someone yells, down below in the street, and the pigeon flies away. In the contrast between the dark pigeon and the bright sunlight, the young man's eyes are imprinted with the shape of the bird so that he sees the bird's silhouette every time he blinks. This lasts for a few minutes only, and when his concentration returns the doctor has finished with his examination and dismisses the young man. The young man steps out of the office building and walks into the sunlight and starts walking down the street, past hot dog vendors, pretzel vendors, and newsstands selling pills in little sachets, all kinds of magazines. The headlines say that a famous movie star was arrested for drug possession. The young man stops for a while at an intersection.

He sees a man in a smart suit and a briefcase disappear into a cab and it reminds him of someone he once loved, many years ago.

p a r t   t w o

The Sea of Decaying Kisses

Horehound

My lover Horehound is resting his head on my belly. I can feel his breath skim over the rivulet of hair that sneaks up to my belly button. My lover takes his name from the herb that takes its name from the Egyptian god of sky and light. I can see why. He may be sky, so vast that it stretches from my toes all the way to the outer atmospheres, but he is certainly night to me, a dark sweep, an elegant constellation, some delicate comfort.

Horehound the plant, after taking the name of a god, applied itself to the sheer enterprise of human infirmity. The early Greeks thought it would salve the bite of mad dogs. They soon discovered that the mulched herb did nothing to stop the rabies from invading the unfortunate body, but not before a sizable number of people foamed at the mouth and died from the bite of humankind's best friend. Do we learn from history? Here I am, begging my

Horehound to bite me on my chest as if he were a mad dog and I a teasing child. Wound me, salve me, my sweet Horehound.

Marrubium vulgare. A vulgar name for a useful plant. *Horehound.* A vulgar name for my passion.

It is a passion that I speak of and I do not speak lightly of it. My Horehound came to me out of a crowd in the middle of a June parade. One hundred thousand people, and he comes fire-strong. I approach him pissful. I approach him scant. I approach him wounded. His spice invades my head, soothes far behind my eyes. Horehound the plant, if taken in large amounts, causes an irregular heartbeat. I know how that feels. All Horehound the lover has to do is give me one look and my feet turn to sandbags. All he has to do is kiss me and I am ready to stop traffic on the freeway, fly off buildings, rob banks.

I am queer for my lover's body. Horehound is mescaline-strong. Dazzling as expensive fireworks. One taste of my Horehound's feast and I beg for his tendrils to twine around my genitals like how a bull is primed for a rodeo. I am ready to be ridden until I kneel on the dusty ground, horns to the dirt, begging to be tamed. Tame me, my sweet, my bitter Horehound. Make me grow unfettered around your body, as your namesake grows.

Lie still; let my tongue function as fingertips, my senses of touch and taste meld. Let me be the cartographer of your body. I know how to start: from your left nipple, closer to your heart, where the pump of blood heats that tit more than the other. A more flavourful place to begin, no? Let me suck, childhungry, until it spurts bitter on my tongue, pushing my mission to the hollow under your left arm, again warmer because of your pumping heart. I will nestle in your brush, press my mouth and nose close to your skin, follow the flow of your blood as a paper boat in a storm drain does, force-fully, involuntarily, to your left wrist, kiss your fingers as if they were a sacrament, read the lines in your palm. I will find the oases, the monuments, the dikes, the hells, the battlegrounds of your body so I will know where to hide when you love me or when you fury me.

Horehound the lover is unscented. I can't smell any-thing of him after he leaves my bed or my apartment. This maddens me as I desperately yearn for some scent of him to linger on my body, on my sheets, my pillows, my clothes. Even as we make mad love on the bed on a hot humid night, and between us we soak the sheets, the smell of him disappears when he leaves and I'm left lying in my bed with my face pressed hard into the pillow where his head lay moments ago.

The sense of smell is the strongest sense of the human body. It is the most arbitrary, unpegged, individ-ual. It is the most powerful, as it alone of the five senses has the power to tap into the uncharted bits of the brain that deal with the harsh labour of memory. You may for-get what an old lover looked like, what he sounded like as you made love, what his kisses tasted like, what the skin on his back felt like, but you will always know what he smelt like. One day, oblivious, some scent hits your nose and somewhere deep in your brain you remember that lover. You remember, perhaps, the time you spent making love on the rooftop of your apartment building under a fog lit orange by the streetlights of the projects nearby. Or perhaps the time you had an argument and how the air smelt like a gourmet stuffed grouse in the oven. The point is, *you remember.*

I smell my hands. Nothing of him remains. Not even my cat can smell him, otherwise she wouldn't crawl into my bed and curl up in the crook of my knee. She's possessive, that cat. She likes my lover because he doesn't intrude into her territory of me. I sniff my sheets frantically. Nothing. My Horehound doesn't give me even this much to placate me until our next meeting. Funny. Horehound the plant is known to unclog one's nose so as to allow a person to breathe easier, to smell more vividly.

These days, we know that hidden in the menthol pierce of horehound the plant lies the cure to soothe a hoarse throat. The decongestive qualities of horehound have been known for centuries. When the tomb of King Tutankhamen was cracked open in late 1922, buried among the urns of treasures and jewels were vats of spices and herbs. One of the jeweled urns contained 100 pounds of dried horehound. Perhaps the king had allergies. All this is useful information for when I approach Horehound the lover.

Under the cheap thrift-store sheets, Horehound and I are trying to find a small island to live on. He takes off his shirt and we have sex. My Horehound is not a man of the printed page. He understands the power of speech. He understands the power of speaking. How the words hang in the air, reflect into my ear, vibrate on my eardrum, and are gone except for the utter pleasure of hearing his voice again. He knows that I will hang on to any and everything he says to me. He knows that I would go to extremes to have him, but he doesn't use that knowledge. He's cruel, that lover of mine: He gives me my freedom.

We are different as night and day, we are, my Horehound and I. I have to rip my throat out to speak his language. In the human body, the ear, nose, and throat are all connected intimately. Each is dependent on the other. Sometimes, a sore throat filled with phlegm will cause an earache and you lose your sense of balance. Horehound has to rip his ears out to hear my language. Ripping your ears out will cause you extreme dizziness. Ripping your throat out will cause your neck to cave in. But that's what we boys do to talk. We're talkers, you see, we talk our boy's talk, boys talking men's talk; we talk until we're hoarse and we listen until we can't stand up without the room spinning like the teacup ride at a county carnival. But does it do any good?

Words are a strange thing. Actually, the English language is a strange thing. All those damn definitions for one plain word. It's such a hotbed of misunderstandings, a cavernous pit of concealment, so prone to debility, deception, heartache. Yikes, did I say *heartache*? Since when have I become some pink and yellow rose-covered airport romance? Since when have I gotten so frightened of mere words?

My Horehound asks me why I love him. It is evening. We are lying in my bed. The sun has set and the sky outside is getting darker in shades. Soon we shall both be lying in darkness, or near darkness, as neither of us is able to reach the lamp switch.

What do I love about my Horehound? It's passion, but more than that. Passion is such an overwrought word. Anything these days that smacks of some semblance of lust is suddenly *passion,* and huge Chinese flares explode in the background, the Earth's crust shatters, and stars fall. Don't people realize they're bastardizing that last true word in the vocabulary of romance? Perhaps I am being selfish. Right, go ahead then, take my word, take *passion,* take it and use it as a piece of Lego. Stack it on top of *love, sex, hot, desire, lust, long-term relationship, significant other.* Make a neat little house with a tidy yard, shuttered windows, and a faithful mongrel crapping on the coconut-husk welcome mat.

Take my word, take *passion,* I don't need it, I'll just leave a blank where it should be; after all, the thing about my [   ] with my lover Horehound is that he reinvents the word for me. So I can't call it [   ] anymore, can I? I could, but it wouldn't be fair, nor would it be correct, and I do so want to be accurate these days. It's a factor of my aging, I guess. Let's just say that my Horehound takes me to a place so incredibly wild and pretty. It's a place where I feel horridly safe. It's good to feel safe but safety always reminds me of danger, otherwise it wouldn't exist. That's my [   ] for him. And his for me? I don't know. All I know is he has an intense passion for his living. But the thing that stuns me is that his passion is so tender. A tender passion can be quite alluring. My [   ] is of him, and his passion is of his life, and I am in his life. Indirect, no?

Once, I accused an ex-lover of not loving me as much as I loved him. "But," he countered, "no one can ever love each other equally." He had a Ph.D., and then I thought that comment made sense. Looking back now, I should have just kicked him in the shins. Okay, maybe it's true, there's no scale to measure the equivalence of passion. And even if there were, most of the time it would be using fingernails in one pan to balance a woolly mammoth in the other. Still unfair.

Passion. It's just a word, and one should never be afraid nor critical of mere words. But then, we boys take what we can get our hands on, what we can put our lips to.

We talk. We kiss. We make love. We have sex. We make love. We talk. We eat dinner. We sleep. We shower. We talk. We have sex. We make love. We buy records together. We talk. We visit. We talk on the telephone. We watch TV. We make love. We talk. We wonder why we bother. We talk.

When Horehound is away from me, I get antsy. I get

nervous and wonder if he's thinking of me as I am thinking of him. I imagine him spelling my name out with crinkle cut fries at the restaurant he works at. When we first met, in the swirl of our first romance, he told me that he had no desire to have sex with anyone else but me. That was a great surprise for him to feel like that, he said, being the slut that he was. Horehound has given me my freedom; I begrudgingly give him his. It's difficult for me to imagine my lover touching another man's body as he touches my body. There can't be too many different ways to touch another body. He says that much of his sexual activity with others has to do with the act, not the emotion; but I know that sex has a way of evoking emotion. How many people have fallen in love because of a good fuck? I suspect that there are people who have dumped their lovers for a better fuck. It's a scary prospect. Once, after a friend of mine was dumped for a better fuck (so he told me), he was spotted slouched in a small café swallowing cup after cup of tepid espresso while writing revenge poems on napkins. I simply refuse to be that tragic.

The flowers of the Horehound attract bees, but the plant only flowers in the second year of its life. Don't expect the little buzzing fellows for a while. There is a story about the beautiful flower who refused to let moths pollinate it. It held out for butterflies only. Whenever it saw a moth approaching, it pulled its petals in until it was a tight little bud. The problem was that the butterflies that followed behind the moths—for butterflies are slow flyers, burdened by the weight of so much useless beauty—saw only an unblossomed bud, and so they passed the beautiful flower. Soon, all the other flowers were pollinated and their petals started to wither and fall, their stamens and ovaries hardened and became fleshy fruit. The beautiful flower, however, remained a beautiful flower. Then a goat came along and ate it.

The first pangs for monogamy bite hard.

Did I expect it to last? Did I expect to be making him pancakes 10 years down the line? Whatever I expected or wanted has been slushed down the septic tank. The unmentionable has happened. That damn talk has gotten me in trouble. He doesn't want to speak a different language anymore. The translations are getting tedious and often cruel, he says. All I ever wanted was for my devotion to be reciprocated, but damn it, devotion and [   ] have done nothing to insulate me from his fear of the ogre of me. Shit, I forgot that the mushy stuff had to work both ways. Am I an ogre? Perhaps. But I'm a lovable ogre.

My friends tell me to let him go, that he was an arsehole to begin with. Jane offers to run him over with her truck; she lives close to him. My friends are protective, they are. They tell me that *I deserve better,* which is the most horrible thing to say to someone who has just been through a breakup instigated by the other. Anyone in similar straits would be ready to downgrade, shop at the K-Mart of Lovers, the factory outlet warehouse sale of desire.

I have chosen to pine. I want him back. I am not beyond groveling. My friends shake their heads with pity. I sometimes think I should know better too, but instead

I'm flinging my heart around on the windy moors like Catherine, desperately pining for my love, only to die of consumption. Yes, in France I would be known as *le faggot pathetique*. As I wandered the Parisian boulevards, I would be mocked and ridiculed with a venom reserved only for American stand-up comedians.

My Horehound has left me and I am suffering. I could douse my aching heart with the distilled water of roses or a stout meal of Gillofloure cloves, both of which are known to strengthen the heart, but why would I mock my heart with the essences of such crass romantic staples? I could mix dried feverfew into sweet wine and sip it through the day; that would cure the vertigo of my loss, but it would only spite the *melancholique* of my poor poor heart. Besides, those are June-July remedies, and it is now September. And even if they were in season and they did work, I would still miss the heady rush, the woody warmth of my Horehound. No, I shall resist every tea. *Gerard's Herbal* will hold no spell over me. I am suffering. I am suffering.

Before the bite of dogs, horehound was thought to save one from the bite of snakes. You would have thought that the Greeks, so capable of philosophy, arithmetic, and medicine, would have deduced that horehound did nothing to soothe the pain of any bite, given the failed rescues of snake bites. Trial and error, do or die.

If I were a rattan snake, so named for the camouflage of my namesake, I would hide in my lover's favourite wicker chair, wait patiently for him to come home, and rest in his familiar comfort. I would stretch forward and chomp him on the back of his calf where the meat is fleshiest and flexed to the fullest when one is in the seated position. I would wait for him to fall to the ground in surprise. As the poison took hold, I would chomp into the arteries on the left side of his neck and suck his blood. I would delight in having his blood flow into my alimentary system, his blood absorbed into my blood, his life my nutrition, his life my hunger. When I drank my fill, I would curl up on his belly, rest my head on the bed of hair that sneaks up to his belly button, wait for my crime to be discovered, and take without flinching what they do to snakes who dare bite humans.

Buildings Go Down

I do not understand buildings that skip the 13th floor. Obviously, the 13th floor still exists, only now it's called the 14th Floor. It's like building planned suburban communities of semidetached houses over an Indian cemetery and then being surprised when the poor hapless denizens, computer programmers and their families, are freaked out when zombies burst into their living rooms and pick at their children's brains.

You step into your office on the 70th floor. You walk across the lobby, greeting the receptionist. You go to the Mr. Coffee to get a cup of coffee. You go to your office, sit down, read the paper, and begin your day without realizing that you are contained in a structure weighing hundreds of tons. A structure that was carefully calculated, measured, and computed so that it all fits together like an old gear watch. The creators have to calculate the tensile strength, how things bend in the wind, expand in heat, contract in cold, bend under weight. They have to plan for when things, living or not, move into the building and across the floor. It is a great responsibility. One of the few times in life when precision and prophecy work in harmony.

I'm told that an earthquake's force on a building grows in proportion to the weight of the structure and the square of its height, and that sand greatly magnifies that force. It's really useless information to me, but somehow I feel good knowing it.

My parents hate that I live in San Francisco. They're scared of earthquakes. With typhoons, floods, and hurricanes at least you get some warning, they tell me, but with earthquakes you could be shitting with a magazine and the next thing you know the whole house has fallen down on you.

We have a small earthquake. My mother calls. Eighteen time zones away, she's read about it. She's worried. She has this image of buildings collapsing all around me, people ducking under cars for shelter, huge cracks on Market Street swallowing people, vendors, vehicles. Her knowledge of earthquakes is the movie starring Steve McQueen in SenseSurround. She thought that movie was a documentary, or at least an educational film. "If an earthquake happens, remember, duck *underneath* a car," she cautioned us after the movie. Similarly, we were told to dive into a pond of water to escape any swarms of attacking killer bees (*The Swarm*), to desperately climb to the rooftop of any burning skyscraper we may be trapped in to get to the rescue helicopter (*The Towering Inferno*), and not to swim in the sea at night because sharks will eat you (*Jaws*).

Back home, all we had to deal with was floods during the monsoon. My grandparents lived in a tin-mining town, and every time there were heavy rains the bombed-out craters, rivers, and mining pools would overflow and the town would flood fast. My grandparents' little zinc-roofed wood-walled house was the highest structure in the town. The house was built on the side of a mountain, on pure rock. The only things that grew well in that soil were pomelo trees. Just sheer luck that they ended up with that plot of land. Even in the worst floods, when the waters were more than 10 feet high and all their neighbours' houses were washed away, they didn't have to evacuate. One monsoon, the pressure of the floodwaters crashed through the front door of their next-door neighbours' house, swept up all the furniture, every single unhinged object, and washed it all out through the back door. My grandparents knew not to worry much. They just waited until the waters subsided, leaving nothing but five feet of thick brown mud littered with dead dogs, cats, goats, and hogs.

Newton had a theory about the attraction between two bodies: the product of the mass of the two bodies, the distance squared, something like that. He used it to explain the planets, gravity, how we stand and walk across the face of the earth, how things come together.

We go to the opera. He says that the Opera House is a gorgeous building, and that it's most beautiful when it is dead quiet. As we walk along the marble and stone corridors, he quietly touches the walls, the pillars that we walk past. To the other patrons, it looks like he's trying to support himself, some kind of difficulty in walking, some connection to his limp. But I know different.

I am reading about the predicted end of the world as detailed in the Book of Revelations. According to Bible scholar Hal Linden, the end will be near when the Temple of Jerusalem is rebuilt on the exact location where it was torn down. The exact location is where the Kaaba now stands in the Great Mosque at Mecca. Every day, thousands of devout Muslims walk around the rock three times, praying. I told Lisa that the moment that rock falls and the construction of a brilliant temple starts, I'll reconvert, repent. In the meantime, I refuse to believe in sin.

A hotel collapsed on the day that I took my SATs, years ago. There were no tremours, no wind, no blast, no explosion, no warning. The entire structure—a four-story hotel, the bank on the first floor and the underground parking lot—just fell down like a deck of cards. The rescue teams worked for days to get to the people trapped under the rubble. In the end, they managed to rescue as many people as they could but had to stop, as the dead bodies pinned under the building were beginning to decompose in the equatorial heat and humidity. The rescue stopped, the volunteers went home, the McDonald's team who showed up to feed the rescue workers packed their Styrofoam containers and tanks of cola into the back of their pickups, and the firetrucks moved in to fill the crushed pile of brick, cement, and metal sitting in the crater with water, to hold the decomposition in something fluid.

Years later, I read about the incident in *Readers Digest*'s Drama in Real Life section. The rescue teams had to cut right through a few dead people in order to get to the living, the story said. Sacrifice the dead for the living, saw right through tough bones and tendons, aim toward the voices crying for salvation.

The government commission that formed to investigate the incident laid the blame on the owner, who did not get some cracks in the walls checked out. The owner died in the collapse. The results were published in the state-owned paper, and everything was fine again. Buildings went up, bigger hotels and convention centers were built, but the lot where that hotel stood lay untouched, a hole in the ground with concrete walls, filled with greenish water, overgrowth, weeds, and strange ripples that surfaced every so often.

Then the economic upturn happened, and the boom of bank vaults and cash registers trumped superstition. The plot of marsh, monument to tragedy and unspeakable deaths, is now a parking structure—$3 per hour until 9 P.M., then $2 until 7 A.M.—and a United Overseas Banking Corporation branch with six 24-hour ATMs.

In the 1440s, Filippo Brunelleschi built the dome of

the Santa Maria del Fiore cathedral in Florence without a scaffold. The dome is supposedly the most difficult construction, a fitting cap to a monstrously complicated building, one wrong calculation and the whole dome would slip right into the building, falling right through the hole it was made to cover.

In July 1945, a B-25 slammed into the 79th floor of the Empire State Building. The impact ripped the wings off the plane and threw one engine right through the building and out the other side, down onto the street. The other engine fell into an empty elevator shaft. Shrapnel from the crash severed an elevator cable and sent the car carrying two women crashing down from the 75th floor to the first. The freefall was broken by machinery and cables in the way, and the two women were seriously hurt but lived. Later, they found out that the plane hit the building's column straight-on, bending the column only slightly. If it had crashed a foot up or down, the Empire State Building from the 79th floor up would perhaps have slid off as if King Kong had swatted it with his hairy paw.

In 1977, a helicopter accident on top of the Pan Am Building sent a chunk of helicopter blade spinning downward into the pavement, killing a man.

When we first met, he took me to a restaurant he designed. There was a built-in brewery in the restaurant. It was Tuesday night, the restaurant was filled with yuppies, and I felt uncomfortably underdressed in my outdated leather jacket and T-shirt. We walked around the building. He took delight in showing me what was where: kitchen, bar, serving station, where the beer comes straight from the distilling tanks right to the tap, where the gas pipes come and go.

Over beer, we talked about something and he said, "Knock on wood." I reached out and rapped on the pillar stretching diagonally from our table. He laughed and said, "That's steel." I sheepishly laughed and looked for some wood with which to redeem myself. Found some in the table. "Is this wood?" I jokingly checked with him. He said yeah but I knew he was wondering what he was doing with someone who can't even tell the difference between wood and metal.

I'm in a building, my body lifted tens of feet off the ground, where it should be. I'm not where my body's natural state lies and the earth calls me to it: some sort of gravitational attraction, something Newton said and Einstein improved upon. I have to trust the physics and the specificity of the beams and support, the predictions of where I would be even before they knew I was going to be there, walking across the floor. Sometime before I was even there, someone said that a 125-pound man will be here and it will be all right. He will be safe. The building will hold him. We'll calculate him in the scheme of things—though they probably predicted someone bigger, much bigger. I like to carry myself bigger, taller than I really am. It's fine until I need to get something off the top shelf or get out of some scrap. *I will build a structure that will hold him up.*

It all lifts me up, a few feet nearer to the conventional wisdom of where God is. I am an inhabitant of the Tower of Babel, obsessed with getting closer to the heavens, waiting to be cursed with the sounds of many languages. I tend to trust everything that can hold me up.

Buildings fall: Structures collapse with little warning, things smash into them, natural disasters strike, the ground sags, people blow them up for profit or protest, they get destroyed in warfare. They get old, redundant, unfashionable, unsafe, they get demolished in a spectacular show broadcast live after prime time. But there's a small-framed man somewhere out there, a man who I once kissed and who did not kiss me back, who tries to get them to stay up no matter what; 125 pounds versus 125 tons, deciding where people stand, where people gather, where people find refuge, where the air belongs, and where the network of it all bridges together.

The Swedish Psychologist

Who is he? Why are you talking to him? Do you know him? and I feel the sting of the backhand across the side of my head. *You're no good, you're nothing but a cheap prostitute. I don't want to see you anymore,* and I'd be on the floor wishing for a bit more wine and pleading with him to not leave me *give me a chance to explain* and that I love him, which must mean something.

He's disappeared to the restroom. He thinks I didn't see the glances that the two have been giving each other the whole night. Hours of mild flirtation and suddenly they're both in the restroom at the same time. "I didn't chase after him in the toilet," he says. "We talked, yeah, we talked." The man wandering around alone is French-Vietnamese, a flight attendant. "Nothing happened; he's good-looking but so are you. Don't you trust me?"

The next week, they are both in Saigon and the French-Vietnamese flight attendant is playing tour guide, showing him the sights, driving him wherever he wants to go, letting him stay at his apartment, cooking for him. In the man's apartment overlooking the sea, he writes me the tenderest love letter he has ever written. He tells me that he loves me dearly, that I will always be dear to him, that he thinks of me all day, that I deserve good things, only the best, to happen to me because I'm special.

I love him so dearly I think I'll kill myself if he ever leaves me. Kill myself like the guy before me that he left for me. The guy's name was Alfie. Alfie in Jakarta. He shows me a picture of the boy. Alfie the Dancer posing by a tree on the beach in the bright June sun, shirt unbuttoned, staring straight at the camera, smiling straight at me. Alfie the Dancer with the new moves he created for some TV variety show. Alfie the Dancer who dances every night so well at the disco. Alfie the Dancer in Jakarta who slashed his wrists to stop *him* from getting on the plane to fly to me.

But he got here and he's in the shower telling me all this. I'm sitting on the toilet bowl, looking at his blurred shape behind the shower curtain, and I love him all the more for coming to me.

I can't take you anywhere. I saw you looking at him. Don't deny it. I just can't trust you. Get out. Stop playing these fucking games with me. Get out. (whack, whack, whack)

I write long letters to him. He sends me an assortment

of long letters and terse postcards. One day, he asks me to dump everything and move to Sweden with him. It is the first time I ever said no to anything he wanted and in my silence and hesitation, I know I've lost him. I know I failed his cruel test.

Everybody wants him, because he's so goddamn good-looking, and they get jealous when we kiss right there in public in the middle of the dance floor. When he puts his tongue in my mouth, I can hear the snide remarks mixed in with the disco music and the metallic hi-NRG break-beats. Everybody loves him and everybody hates me.

I can't believe you'd go out with someone who looks like that. How can you go with someone so ugly and then go with me?

He's old enough to be my father. We're sitting at the airport lounge waiting for his plane to Bali when I mention this fact to him and we laugh about it. *Let's say that I'm your son; you were in Vietnam and I'm your adopted son,* I say. From then on, every letter began *Dearest son...*

I love this man so much and there's nothing more perfect than sitting on a train with him, traveling thousands of miles, and me leaning my head against his body all night long. Later, we're lying on the beach in the darkness, the stars not bright enough to light anything, the moon nowhere in sight, and he fucks me. "We need to make memories for ourselves," he says.

He sends me two cassette tapes. Ry Cooder and Bette Midler.

The songs on the Ry Cooder Tape are:

SIDE A
634-5789
Why Don't You Try Me?
Down in the Boondocks
Johnny Porter

SIDE B
The Way We Mend a Broken Heart
Crazy 'Bout an Automobile
The Girls From Texas
Borderline
Never Make Your Move Too Soon

The songs on the Bette Midler tape are:

SIDE A
Is It Love?
Favorite Waste of Time
All I Need to Know
Only in Miami
Heart Over Head

SIDE B
Let Me Drive
My Eye on You
Beast of Burden
Soda and a Souvenir
Come Back Jimmy Dean

The song on the first side of the Bette Midler tape, "All

I Need to Know," that's our song, he says when we meet up later. He takes a pen out of his pocket, takes the tape out of my hands, pulls the cassette sleeve out, and circles the title of the song. "I don't know much, but I know that I love you, and that's all I need to know," he croons with the passion of the most seasoned karaoke crooner.

I take Polaroids of him. Silly artsy pictures that I sign and date. Him lying on the white hotel bedspread, arm behind his head, bare-chested, in white trousers. Him standing silhouetted against the window, the crack of his arse and his tan line just creeping out of the shadows. He takes many pictures of me too. I find them later when I'm going through his bags. Many of the pictures were taken when I was sleeping, curled in the big hotel bed, where he pulled the sheets down so he could see my buttocks, my limp cock, my arm folded recklessly across my body. Then, I was young enough and foolish enough to find these pictures charming and was actually quite flattered.

Alfie finds them one day, starts screaming hysterically, grabs the tailoring shears and cuts them up into little pieces, screaming "He's disgusting! He's disgusting!" over and over again. He calms the poor boy down with kisses and a good long fuck.

My colleague at the restaurant I'm working at finds the picture that I keep of him with me. "He's so handsome," she shrieks and asks to give her a copy of the photograph. She is 16 and has bagged herself an American scuba instructor. It was between him and the Italian businessman. One day, the Italian shows up at the club where she is drinking with her friends and wants her to go back to Milan with him. She says "Okay!" and tells him to wait by the door while she says her goodbyes. When she gets to the door 10 minutes later, he's gone, and he never comes back, so she ended up with the American who paid for her to have a complete blood test. "Thirty-two strains of V.D.," she tells me, *"all clean."* The American doesn't want her to work, but what else is there to do now that she can't go out on dates, she moans. "Before I went and got married, every day I go on dates!"

We're sitting in a cafe on Orchard Road having baguettes and cappuccinos, discussing Kafka's *The Trial* and some silly modern art exhibition we saw a few days ago. He loves discussing these things with me, he says; he just can't do that with Lek, his new friend in Bangkok. I accuse him of cheating on me. But Lek is not like any of the other boys in Bangkok. "He's shy, quiet, and has this great smile; when he's with me, he doesn't look at anyone else on the street, not like you. But we're just friends; we're not sleeping together."

Two weeks later, we're checked into a cheap hotel on Bencoolen Street. In the glow of the dirty orange carpet and the frosted green windows, he says to me, "Why do you need any KY? Lek doesn't, he just lets me put it in with spit. He does it so much better than you, you could learn from him."

Two days later, Dr. Hans Linden finishes his research in cross-cultural psychology in Bangkok and returns to Växjo. I leave for America. It is two days before my 18th birthday, and I spend both of them alone in a hostel room watching MTV. George Michael's "Monkey" is number 1 for the second week in a row.

Opercuthalousas (A Lexicon for Blindness)

AFFECTION. There are many ways to go blind: Diseases, accidents with sharp prongs, hereditary conditions, serious masturbation, affection.

Bondage. When you go blind, your other senses become more intense. Smell, touch, hearing, and taste intensify. Your lover's tongue in your ear sounds like a hissing hurricane, its wet slab sliding around your lobe feels like an amorous eel that will slip into your mouth; and even before that moment, you smell him approaching. The idea of hooding someone who you have sex with is to achieve this heightened sensitivity. Elaborate blindfolds and hoods made of silk, leather, metal, or rubber have been invented for this purpose. Simple silk sashes wrap around your eyes, their delicious cool material hangs down the back of your head, tickling the nape of your neck; the more elaborate ones made of leather, metal, or rubber employ straps and buckles, buttons and ties, strategically placed airholes and gags to grip a person's face in anticipation of the utter pleasure of feeling.

CUNNING. But do we need to feel anything so intensely? Or is it just a frill of life. The extra gooey topping on the sundae at 50 cents more. Mere fluff to our senses, our bodies.

DEADLOCK. Even then, this pleasure is only temporary. If you're deprived of your senses for too long, you will start to get quite crabby, irritable at any stimulus. People lifted out of isolation tanks have been known to snap and become quite violent at the first people they see.

Sensory pleasures were always considered a sin. Better you should dull your senses with painkillers, but even that may be such a pleasure.

EPIPHANY. You see when light is reflected off of something. This light passes through the lens of the eye and is projected on the retina at the back of the eyeball. The muscles of the eye will contract and expand accordingly to focus the image. The projected image is inverted in the retina, but the brain rights the image and we see what it is we see.

FANCY. Modern lobotomies are performed through the eye. No more shaving the head, hewing off the skull, and slicing the brain. No more little partitions that allow the surgeons to work solely on the crown of a head, never seeing the face of the patient. No more unsightly scars and tight Frankensteinesque stitches across the head. Only blurred sight from one eye.

GENEALOGY. I once had a lover who had the most gorgeous tattoos. While he slept, I would lie beside him and watch the curve of the dark pattern flick its way down his arm. By all intents and purposes, the affair should have worked out: Our tattooists were best friends, his piercer went to the same political focus group that I went to, we shaved our heads in almost the same cycles, we smoked our rooms with the same incense.

HOMOGENOUS. The first time I went down on him, the scent of patchouli that he had dabbed just under his belly button gripped me hydra-like, and I wanted to fall asleep on his belly.

IDOLATRY. Of course, we didn't make it past two weeks. I blame him totally.

Once the blame has been assigned, the healing can begin.

JEZEBEL. A month later, I found out that he was shacked up with a tile salesman from Colma who was an actor on the side. They moved in together after only two and a half weeks and were in the initial throes of domestic bliss. They were looking to adopt a dog, a friend who works at the pound told me.

I often find myself wondering what their bathroom looks like.

KISMET. Describe your pleasure. It's difficult, isn't it? That's why we have poetry, Hallmark, stand-up comics, and dictionaries. That's why we have a brain that can store random bits of information, like the part of the body your lover last kissed before leaving you, and how that one spot feels different from the rest of your body for the rest of your life.

LUXURY. Under the circumstances, I can see how I can be smitten by something so epidermal as tattoos on a man. Perhaps it's the way the markings lurk underneath all those layers of skin, sneaking between muscle and glassy epidermis, brilliant colours visibly lurking in such microscopic depths.

MANIA. What I desire and what I end up with are two vastly different things. Ripe and raw; school buses and dingoes.

NAUSEA. Did I mention we both cooked a mean dinner?

OPERCULUM. When you look at food, you see the fleshy chunks of meat, the crisp inviting vegetables, or the appetizing wheat moulded into something far from its grainy origins. When you smell food, it literally hits you right between the eyes. It possesses your whole body, your mind kicks in, and you desire the smell to melt on your tongue, your memory kicks in to compare the taste with others like it stored in your head. Your arms ache to bring the food to your mouth. Your ears ache to hear the clink of cutlery and the subsequent grinding of your teeth against one another and the slivers of food, that sound of chewing only your ear can hear.

PROVIDENCE. As much as the big eye-catching ingredients elicit such responses in you, it is the small things in the food, the stuff that blends into the food that gives it flavour, that gives it the tang which makes you want to weep with joy, laugh until your belly aches, or that sours your face up.

Spices disappear into the dish almost, covered and marred by the obtrusive masters they were employed to serve. The powdered spices vanish, the grainy spices soften and wilt, but not before bleeding their colour and their scent into the dish.

QUANTUM. When a corpse is to be mummified, a wire hanger is inserted into the corpse's nose until it hits the skull cavity. The corpse's brain is dragged out by the hooked wire hanger. The body must be dried thoroughly and any membrane or organ that is not sheer muscle, raw flesh must be removed or it will decompose and create moisture, hence damaging the delicate desiccating process. Any leftover brain is taken out via the eye socket, a much wider passageway than the nostril; the eyes—removed much earlier—are replaced with shiny pearls, the brain cavity filled with dried flowers, aromatic leaves, and herbs.

In the afterlife, the body opens its eyes and sees only the brightest jewels, smells the greatest scents.

RESTITUTE. In history, certain spices were revered as treasures. But now you can go to a 24-hour supermarket and simply chuck a small bottle into your cart, totally oblivious that it is a powerful historic artifact.

SHROUD. Take saffron. It takes 80,000 saffron flowers to obtain an ounce of saffron. Thus, it was originally used as a religious ash by Buddhist monks. Only the monks in the monastery were allowed to grow, harvest, and make it. Once thought to be exclusive to the religious orders and the highly pious, saffron found its way to the masses after visitors to a group of monks proclaimed that the blessing of this wondrous flower be shared.

TAMPER. Saffron stains horribly. Once it touches cloth, the fabric takes on the orange colour of saffron forever. The monks who harvested and made the spice would often wipe their hands on their robes, hence creating what are known today as saffron robes. But think back to the wondrous smears of colour and scent on the monks as they made their way along the streets, begging for alms and giving a hint of saffron to the people to put into their rice pots so that in the evening everyone would have the lovely surprise of opening a pot and being greeted by the delicious smell, a tasty treat, an ordinary everyday meal transformed.

UNCOMMITTED. There are spots on the retina where images, after passing through the lens of the eye, do not reflect, hence the image never appears in your brain. The light rays and the image enter the watery mass of your eyeball and simply vanish. This is known as the blind spot. Something dangling right in front of your eyes may not ever be seen by you.

VISION. Passion and astigmatism.
Here I go blindly stumbling barefoot through the bamboo-shoot jungle.

WISH. I have a fantasy where a man obsessed with me would secretly live in my basement and sneak into my apartment when I'm away or asleep. He leaves china cups, pressed flowers, and insects preserved in vodka in small jam jars where I will find them. In my bathtub, he leaves small sculptures of cranes that he carves out of carrots and cucumbers. I pretend that all these objects appearing in my apartment are nothing out of the ordinary so he will continue doing it. On the 90th day, I will leave a trail of paprika leading to a sheet of glass with my thumbprint on it for him.

X. It's perfectly all right to skip over something. The eye does it if the object is close enough to the face.

YEARNING. One spice that you must know of is cumin, a fine grainy spice. It is sold in supermarkets either as a powder or as seeds. It is used commonly in Middle

Eastern and Indian dishes. To release the smell and flavour of the whole seed, the seeds are placed in the palm and rubbed vigourously. It is said that cumin was favoured as an aphrodisiac in a certain Sultan's reign. He demanded that handfuls of it be used in the preparation of his and his wives' and concubines' meals. His servants and cooks spent all day furiously rubbing away, their palms all sore and raw from the friction of the seed. Their hands permanently stained with the smell of cumin.

ZEALOT. If any of the kitchen helpers accidentally brought their odour-stained hands to scratch their back or rub their belly, that part of the body would immediately be stained with the same heady smell.

When they went home, they only needed to brush their partners' hair with their hands and their partners immediately got aroused. The servants who were single needed only present their hands to their romantic interest and the person would simply swoon.

It's amazing to think that you can lean into someone's hands, rest your head on someone's pot belly, and fall so hopelessly in love.

The French Ambassador

It had been raining unceasingly for weeks. The kind of rain that falls alternately in spells of big heavy drops and then in a fine spray that spirals like dust guided according to the wind's breath. Either way, the sound of the droplets of water hitting the surfaces of everything stayed in your mind and in your ears no matter where you were. No matter how dry you were, that unceasing sound always made you feel damp. It was nothing unusual though. It was Singapore in December: monsoon season. An umbrella did nothing to keep the everchanging direction of rain off you and the plastic raincoats only trapped the humid air and condensed it between the plastic and your flesh, making your skin shiver with the warm damp.

It was like this the year before and the year before that and every year since anyone could remember, but for the ambassador the climate is horrendous and wholly oppressive. He hates the rain. He hates everything about it, especially how the sounds seem to follow him everywhere he goes. He tells me that he thinks he will go mad with the sound. I know what he means, but I pretend that I don't hear anything. Know more than you let on, that's how I came to him, how I stayed with him, and that's how I left.

He picks me up at a shopping mall. I am taken by his accent and his weathered good looks. We seem to get along very well. He asks me to his house, to stay for a while. I tell my parents that I'm staying at a friend's, something about studying a lot for my upcoming mock GCE O levels. They buy it and I spend a lot of time at his government-supplied mansion not doing anything, and I like it.

He hates it if my cock is hard. He can barely stand to look at it. It disgusts him and he turns away, leaves the room almost immediately. Sometimes he turns me over and makes me lie on my stomach so that he can't see the offensive piece of muscle. He likes my cock soft and shrunken, to stay unawakened no matter how much he touches and kisses it. Some days, I take to releasing myself in the bathroom, two or three times a day, in preparation for him in the evening.

He likes touching me. He likes running his fingers and the palms of his hand all over me as if I were a small fleshy toy. He loves the smooth curves of my body. He makes me lie down on his big bed and he kneels between my legs. He lifts me so that my buttocks rest on his lap and he runs his hands all over my body, feeling my chest, my nipples, my shoulders, my stomach, especially my legs. They're strong legs, I know that. When you're short, small-framed, and light, you need a part of your body you can count on; for me, it's my legs. He tells me that they are the most feminine part of my body, that's why he adores them so. Men have strong shoulders, strong arms, but women, they have strong strong hips and legs, that's where they are most powerful, he tells me. He has neither. He is skinny, fragile. I know that if I grab him in a scissor lock between my thighs, I can crush his ribs, like a child smashing a cracker for fun, all in one deliberate, cruel, and careless squeeze.

Lie on your stomach, he says again, overpowered by his need for my soft, childlike, harmless cock. "I wish I could cut it off for you," he whispers once while he is playing with my body. I pretend I didn't hear him but the thought that one day he might just grab a pair of shears and rip my cock off my body scares me so much that I shudder. He mistakes my trembling as a response to his hands and he is excited, happy, and he accidentally ejaculates, the first time I ever see him do it. He's embarrassed by his stray act. He apologizes, and I actually feel sorry for him. He doesn't like me to see him erect then fading away like that. I feel it often enough but seeing it is another matter. His cock collapses and shrivels up almost instantly, the last white drops barely flowing when it all retracts into folds of skin.

No, I never see him ejaculate, he doesn't let me. When he puts me on my stomach and starts rubbing my back I can feel his cock rubbing against the crack of my buttocks. I feel his cock stiffening, then pressing. He never tries to force his way into me. With his cock, he likes to accidentally press against me, and I feel his fingers and palms running up and down my back while his cock bumps against me. Then I feel a short spurt of wetness and I know he's done.

Another thing he likes is bathing me. He brings me to the shower and puts me under the hot spray and soaps me, washing every crevice in my body he can put his fingers into. He likes the water hot. As he soaps me, he slowly turns the tap, making the water hotter and hotter until my flesh turns a blush red and his every touch leaves streaks of white on my slowly blanching flesh.

Then he towels me dry, rubs skin lotion all over me, and brings me to the big wooden bed he shipped all the way from France.

The housekeeper and I become friends. When he's out, we sit in the kitchen, drink tea, eat biscuits, and talk. She tells me that he is repulsed by the local people. He wanted to be posted to Belgium or Sweden or anywhere in America, but somehow he ended up on the equator in a country he didn't even know how to pronounce correctly. He thinks the local people are filthy, she tells me. "When I first came to work for him, he make me show him my hands. He check my fingernails. He say there's where germs always hide. In the fingernails. Then he go buy this special soap, antiseptic, and he tells me that I have to bathe every day in it and wash my hands every hour with it." Then there was the first gardener. "One day, Sir looks out the verandah and he see the gardener chewing sireh and spitting the juice out on the ground, and Sir become so angry. He fire the gardener on the spot, and then Sir become sick. Fever and vomiting, and he hires someone to spray the whole garden, and he still hates to walk in the garden."

The housekeeper and I never talk about what I'm doing there. She knows: She has to handle the sheets after he finishes with me.

I ask him to walk in the garden with me. He says he's discovered that he's allergic to the carpet grass since he first came here. I tell him that's silly: People get allergic to the weed-like crab grass, not the luxurious special-ordered carpet grass. He says that he's European, that Europeans have more sensitive skin, not only to grass but also to sun. He won't even perform official duties if it involves exposing his flesh to grass during some function, he says.

One Wednesday night, his wife shows up. We're in his room and he's playing me a video of his favourite French entertainer, some French version of Shirley Bassey, and we hear a taxi pull up. He greets her at the door, kisses her on the cheek. Actually, he tries to kiss her on the lips but she turns her face and he ends up kissing her wetly on the cheek. She turns, and he kisses her on the other cheek. His tongue leaves a streak in her rouge; he wipes the taste of the powder off on his sleeve. He's surprised to see her, shocked. She's supposed to be home, somewhere in France attending lunches, raising money for charities, and showing up at openings of art galleries and selected operas that their friends are involved with. The housekeeper helps the taxi driver unload bag after bag from the boot of the car. We carry all 23 suitcases to his room. Watching the stream of suitcases, we all know that things will change around the house.

She asks him who I am. He tells her that I'm the housekeeper's son. I'm Chinese and the housekeeper is Malay, but she doesn't seem to notice or to care. She sits on the sofa, puts her feet up on the coffee table and complains about the humidity. "Get me a cold drink, boy," she barks at me. "My mouth is…"—she fishes for the words—"…so dry." I quietly leave the room and go to the kitchen. Her accent is so exotic, the way she speaks, the way she pronounces her words, the way she searches for the right word. The housekeeper makes a tall glass of heavily sweetened iced tea for me to bring to her. He meets me halfway up the stairs and takes the glass from me. He tells me to wait for him in the kitchen.

I've only seen his wife in photographs. In the photographs she looks like some anonymous elegant French lady in prints you see at postcard shops. Mrs. Ambassador with the smart dress, the gloves, and the chic hat, sitting just perfectly and not ever committing the utterly gauche act of looking directly into the camera.

The wife doesn't like me. She cannot understand why I am always in the house. She ignores me, walks right by me. She'd walk right through me if she could. She thinks the Chinese race is hideously deformed, the Muslims even more. She likes Indians, though. She likes how their dark skins look against her fair complexion. The housekeeper is telling me all this. I don't know how she knows. I just know that I believe it to be true simply because I want it to be.

I miss walking around his house in the afternoons when he's not around. The wife is usually sitting on the verandah reading French magazines or having tea with her friends that she met at the Alliance Française. A bunch of socialites, a mix of local and expatriate wives, sipping tea, discussing books, films, shopping, fashion, and interior decorating, and sighing about how you just can't get a good cup of properly brewed tea in the Tropics, not with these hideous Lipton teabags invading the globe.

One day he's at work and the house is quiet. I walk around touching his antiques, dragging my fingertips across the varnished surfaces of the teak tables, leaving a silent streak that fades as quickly as it appears. I rub my knees against the marbled legs of his dining-room chairs, my cheek against the cold porcelain vases. I imagine this is what he feels when he rubs his body against me, runs his hands like a blind piano player on my legs.

I get gripped by the desire to enter his room and sit in his cupboard, letting the smell of his colognes and washes overpower me. I push his bedroom door open, and the crack of light from my act throws a spotlight on our bed, where the wife is nakedly squatting and squirming over an Indian man's lap. His dark skin and her pale skin are dripping with sweat. The Indian man is shocked at the intrusion and utters a cry of surprise. She turns around, looks me straight in the eye, and turns back around to her lover and ignores me as if I were merely a stray cat that wandered into the room. The Indian man laughs and returns to his duties. She is still silently squirming, not even as much as heavy breathing.

She is cheating on him, and I am cheating on him. Damn it, I didn't mean to, but somehow I needed some kind of overt sex act as well, and sex with him was anything but overt. One day, at the same shopping mall, I meet the Assistant German Ambassador, the number 2 German in the country. He takes me back to his office in the consulate, housed on the 30th floor of a tall office building with a departmental store as its base.

The elevator door opens, he steps out cautiously, looks around, and beckons me to follow him. He shows me how to avoid the revolving video camera that records the goings-on around the elevator foyer and the entrance to the consulate.

It is after 6 o'clock and the office is empty. He brings me to his office, where he fucks me in the arse. All I remember is the fabulous view from his office window—the harbour stained with tankers and ships, the green-tiled pagoda from a nearby hotel, the scurrying shoppers dotting Orchard Road—and the fact that he had bad breath.

The second time, he takes me to his house; his wife has taken the kids to soccer practice and won't be back for a while. He leads me in the dark to his room, which smells of mildew and powder, and he fucks me in the arse again. He refuses to turn on the lights because he's scared the neighbours will be suspicious. He still has bad breath. On the way out, my eyes become vaguely accustomed to the dark and I notice a vast collection of Oriental rugs, all rolled up and leaning against the walls, looking like Greek columns, all tagged and ready for shipping. I use my hands to navigate around the rough undersides of rugs and stumble down the stairs. Later, the French Ambassador discovers a nasty scrape on my elbow that I had gotten as I brushed against one of the rough inverted rug pillars. I tell him I got it from falling out of a frangipani tree while trying to pluck a flower for him. He is happy.

The third time, it was the office again. The same stepping around of the video camera. The same dick in my arse. The same foul breath. The same glorious view. This time he tells me about the building the Consulate is housed in, where the security cameras are and how to come into the building and out on any floor without being seen by the guards. The whole building of 56 floors, and I am a ghost, flitting from floor to floor, unseen.

After the third time, I never hear from him again.

The French Ambassador is reposted to Belgium, and he leaves quietly and undoubtedly joyfully. The last time we are together, he wants to put his tongue into my mouth. He has never french-kissed me before, which I think is really funny. He doesn't like kissing because he believes it's the best way the germs that cause those horrid tropical diseases spread. It is the first time I ever kissed a smoker. I always thought I would be repulsed at the taste of stale smoke and nicotine, having seen all too many pictures of lung cancer and the stuff they scrape out of smoker's throats. Surprisingly, the bitter tang of his tongue excites me, and I immediately grow hard. This time he doesn't mind and he even puts his mouth to my cock.

I remember this too: Near his mansion was a huge monsoon drain, one of the many in the city. It had been raining for days still and as I was passing by I heard this loud mewing. In the drain, eight feet deep, was a small ginger-striped kitten stranded on a piece of piping that stretched across the drain. The drain was filled with rushing brown water churning into a dark tunnel under the road. I tried to point out to the kitten where it could put its paws—never mind the cold awful damp feel on its paw pads—to get to safety. But all the poor animal saw was a huge human hanging over the guard railing, hovering over her. I ran to the nearest pay phone and called the SPCA. The voice on the other end of the line told me they'd get there as soon as they could. I went back to the drain to tell the little kitty the news. She was still mewing loudly. Then, suddenly, she just tipped over and fell into the water, as if she were an unstable toy made of granite, and was swept into the dark tunnel. I stood there for more than an hour trying to see if she would crawl out of the tunnel, but neither the cat nor the SPCA ever came.

I went back to his mansion, soaking wet. He was at home reading. Some shrill French chanteuse was on the record player. He asked me what was wrong. I said, "The cat fell into the drain." He said, "You look like you need a bath, my wife is out shopping."

Looking back now, the odds of picking up (or being picked up by) two foreign dignitaries from different countries at the same shopping mall was quite incredible. I imagine Interpol briefing delegates and consul workers about the shopping mall and how to pick up local boys outside the Wendy's.

A month later, a good friend of mine calls me. He is excited and tells me that he had sex with this German guy while the wife and kids were at soccer practice.

"Did he have bad breath?" I ask.

"Yes," my friend says.

So the two ambassadors left without sending for me, without lifting me out of my pathetic existence to come live with them in their splendid mansions in Europe. Just as well, I guess, because I was only 15. I was reading Arthur Miller's *The Crucible* in school for my year-end literature exams. I imagined being brought into court, where I would finger the two as the men who did those shameful acts to me. The power of blackmail, the power of crushing their happy little lives of family and politics simply because I was jealous and I couldn't stand being jilted and left behind. Perhaps I was desperately wanting to be saved but was left with nothing but the clatter of their sad secret lives and the hollow whims of their chaste kisses.

1. You stab yourself.

Sometimes you think the sadness will never end and you fold like a drop of sand caught in the deep furrows of a seashell that some kid in bright-eyed excitement brings home from a seaside sojourn. The fond treasure sits in a special place on the kid's dresser—beside wishing trolls, snapshots, spoiled toys, and hairbrushes—with that drop of sand hidden, but the germs and bacteria contained in that drop move faster than delight.

"I am sending you to them to open their eyes and turn them from darkness to light and from the power of Satan to God, so that they may receive forgiveness of sins and a place among those who are sanctified by faith."

2. You hang yourself.

I have no more rituals left.

3. You jump out of the third-floor window.

I had a friend who would call me in the middle of the night because she believed that there was a spirit in her room and it was trying to push her out of the window. The spirit had no face, just like in the stories we told in primary school in the school bus as the sun was setting. "It's not a druggie flashback, I know what a flashback is," she would say, and then we'd talk for a while until her boyfriend came home from work.

4. You push drawing pins into your thigh.

5. You cut your fingertips with a Bic.

do this: count the rings on the flats of your fingers tips / take a sharp knife and open them up / collect the blood in a chinese soup spoon / use blue porcelain if you can /

your lover will come & say / o, you're into that, are you / you must not say a word / he will take the knife and cut / the shapes of animals onto your shiny stomach / when you move / the animals will masturbate each other / you will laugh and wonder / what it is to feel something good on your sex.

6. You bang your head against the fire iron.

All I know of the man is that he has a raspy cough, the sort old people who smoke too much have. Even though I do not see his tongue, I can tell just by the feel of it on the underside of my cock that it is coated with the layer of green furry mucus that characterizes that cough. I know because the last time, and it was a different person, I saw his face when he looked up, mouth opened, tongue sticking way out, dog-like, in anticipation of some warm jism. "Come's good for the body," he tells me, and he needs it because he's got "a fuckin' bad heart" from working in some shit-arse pissant cleaning job. The harsh chlorine cleaners make his hands rough and his fingernails corrode as if he were a pathological nail-biter. Funny thing, he says, is that he would bite his *fuckin' nails* if he could but now it's too late so he smokes like mad. Nervous habit and it keeps him warm, he says.

7. YOU BITE YOUR THUMB UNTIL IT BLEEDS.

"You are to abstain from food sacrificed to idols, from blood from the meat of strangled animals, and from sexual immorality. You will do well to avoid these things."

8. YOU SHOOT YOURSELF.
shin shin shin shin
shin shin shin shin
shin shin shin shin
shin shin / shin

8A. YOU DRIVE SPLINTERS INTO THE BACK OF YOUR HAND.

The angels in books and Bible stories were always clean-shaven white men. You knew they were men because they didn't have breasts like in old old paintings you see in books about old paintings. And those wings, like big pigeons, as if someone broke the wings off a pigeon and stuck them to those white bodies. The angels always wore slippers—or sandals, as my Sunday school teacher said while retelling Bible stories with local street names so it would be interesting for us, to think that Jerusalem had a 7-Eleven or a McDonald's right around the synagogue. What a mess it would be to walk around in slippers all the time, especially after a good rain, and when you walk, the slippers flick little spots of mud onto the back of your outfit. A real pity—those angels had such white outfits. I wondered, *If Jerusalem had a Safeway, does heaven have a Laundromat?*

8B. YOU WALK INTO ONCOMING TRAFFIC.

One day we did Revelations, and the angels became quite serious. They started flying everywhere with fire and pots of boiling stuff and had strange animal pets and I wondered what happened to those nice clean-shaven white men.

8C. YOU DRINK WEED-KILLER.

Then there was the New Year Eve service. My mother told me that at midnight an angel would appear right above the cross in the tallest part of the ceiling, right at the steeple. I wondered if it would be a nice clean angel or a serious fire angel animal. So I listened to the choir, played with my fingers, read the hymn in *Praise Songs* backward, pinched myself to stay awake. At 11:59 we were supposed to pray, but I peeped.

I never saw the damn promised angel.

9. YOU BURN YOUR CHEST WITH CIGARETTES.

Cigar ashes are much hotter than cigarette ashes. Ashes from a pot stoogie you barely notice. When they tell you that your loved one's ashes are in the urn, they lie. It's mostly scrapings from the inside of the furnace. To be sure, always check for the big bones, the ones that don't burn easy. A real urn would have big bones that look like clean polished ham hocks, and dust, lots of it.

10. YOU STEP BAREFOOT ON BROKEN GLASS.

11. YOU STEP BAREFOOT ON LIVE WIRES.

Sometimes his kisses taste like sand, the kind you accidentally take a tongueful of when you go under the tide and rise, head popping out of the green foam like some marine prairie dog, and the grains rub between your teeth, into your gums, making the sea-salt water sting right into your mouth all along up to the cracks at the sides of your eyes.

12. YOU CUT YOUR BIG TOE WITH A CHEESE-SLICER.

Americans have this fear and loathing of large people. They have the idea that a big man will run up behind them and mug them. Perhaps this is why Americans feel so safe in Asia. There, most people are short and small; what harm can they do? And even if they did try anything, the bigger chap would definitely win, hands down, no contest.

13. YOU WHIP YOURSELF WITH TELEPHONE WIRE.

This is also why so many Westerners try to smuggle drugs through Asian airports. What could those little Asian customs people do? They're so tiny! So short!

Surely they can't have the brains to suspect that I've got 60 kilos of heroin shoved up my long pant leg, my butt, my friend's twat, and in my backpack under my undies, they think.

14. YOU CLUB YOURSELF WITH A PUTTER.

But they are caught and chucked in some rat, roach, and V.D.-infested Third World prison. The newsmagazine cameras come to document their plight, their family poses for tearful pleas to let their Dear Son go free: "He's never done anything like that before! Those short crafty Asians must've set him up," they weep. Sweaty diplomats try to wrangle a deal. A Hollywood film crew comes and makes a movie about the poor bloke's ordeal.

15. YOU WRAP BARBED-WIRE AROUND YOUR WAIST.

In Hollywood movies, the role of Thailand is played by Vietnam. The role of the Phillipines is played by Malaysia. The role of India is played by Singapore. The role of Malaysia is played by Indonesia, or Thailand if necessary. The role of Indonesia is played by Cambodia. The role of Singapore is played by Hong Kong. The role of Vietnam is played by Hawaii, or by Sound Stage Number 8 in Burbank.

16. YOU PUT YOUR FIST THROUGH THE TV SCREEN.

Aileen Wuornos, the Florida highway lesbian serial killer, was 5-foot-4 inches tall. She killed nine men who treated her like shit. Eyewitnesses who remembered her at truck stops and diners said that she was 5-foot-8 inches tall. Aileen Wuornos did not wear stiletto heels.

17. YOU CUT YOUR TONGUE WHILE CHEWING ON RAZOR BLADES.

It is easy to tell who will win on *People's Court* or any of the numerous TV courtroom shows: If you are the better-groomed party, you win. If you are vaguely coloured, you lose. If you look and talk nice, you win. If you have an Afro or long hair and don't wear a good suit, you lose. If you have tattoos or piercings that show, you will definitely lose.

If Aileen Wuornos was on *People's Court* and if (with the help of her new guardian, the born-again Christian woman Arlene Pratt) she did her hair up real nice like Shelley Hack on *Charlie's Angels,* she would be free.

18. YOU POUR BATTERY ACID ON YOUR LEGS.

In the TV movie of her life, the actress that played Wuornos was 5-foot-10 inches tall.

19. YOU POUR BATTERY ACID ON YOUR TESTICLES.

The first time I ever knew of someone else's semen was in a park. I had found a used condom under the bench I was sitting on. I slipped two fingers into the floppy sheath and withdrew them with a sliver of wet on my fingertips that I held up to my nose to smell, but in my jitter I slipped and accidentally wiped it on my lips. It was about 7 in the morning and there were few people about, joggers mostly, so I was sure no one saw me. But the smell of semen stayed in my fingernails for the rest of the day, even as I washed my hands repeatedly.

20. YOU INSERT A TOOTHPICK INTO YOUR URETHRA.
Pain / No pain.

21. YOU STAPLE YOUR EYELID INTO A NEAT FOLD.
Pain / No pain.

22. YOU BURN YOUR LEFT NIPPLE WITH A HOT CURLING IRON.
On *Championship Wrestling*, the sort with fake theatrical names and silly costumes to fill out those names, we are treated to large men pulverizing each other. The slap of flesh against flab, Spandex stretch, and loud, loud, foul curses. I have a theory that if you sat close enough you could smell the men's pheromones, and biologically that would be a turn-on.

23. YOU GET ZINC POISONING.
If Santa Claus did come from the North Pole, he would look more indigenous, more Eskimo, not like a big white bloke. If he merely moved to the North Pole, that would only prove his colonial tendencies. What is more important is what those elves he has enslaved look like. Are they the original inhabitants of the land that Santa invaded?

24. YOU GET STUNG BY CATFISH.
Cats and dogs see spirits that humans do not.
When I walk through my apartment with my cat, we see different things. I see a mess that needs cleaning up,

a stove, a scratching post, a dehydrated plant. My cat sees powerless demons lounging around with nothing to do except sit on the settee and pout and preen.

25. You burn in hell.

According to some Chinese mythology, there are seven levels of hell, each governed by a presiding demon. At Haw Pa Villa, the Tiger Balm Gardens in Singapore, there is a sculpture of hell in which ceramic demons punish ceramic sinners. Liars' tongues cut off, gluttons disemboweled, murderers pierced by meathooks, fornicators dipped in molten sulphur. Parents usually bring their children to see this exhibit to teach them the value of obedience and filial piety. Even Christian parents who do not believe in anything vaguely Buddhist or Taoist will drag their children on sunny Sunday afternoons after Church to witness hell. A person always knew where the exhibit was in the Gardens by following the sound of children wailing and shrieking in fear. There you will find children, red-eyed, shaking, and crying, held firmly by their parents and forced to look at hell. Once, the cleaning crews started work late. The visitors got to watch the tired old caretaker sweep and dust the ceramic hell. This was the only time there was no fear on either side of the glass.

"Let no one cause me trouble, for I bear on my body the marks of Jesus. The grace of our Lord Jesus Christ be with your spirit, brothers. Amen."

26. You burn in heaven.

In the 26th chapter of the Acts of the Apostles, Paul tells the king of Agrippa how he turned from being a sinner, how he met the spirit of the crucified Christ face-on and was transformed to a disciple of goodness and love.

In the 27th chapter of the Acts of the Apostles, Paul sails for Rome, where God saves the ship from a storm.

In the 28th chapter of the Acts of the Apostles, nothing much happens.

A Sea of Decaying Kisses

Anna May Wong is dead. Left on some ice float, lips unkissed. Anna May Wong and Mae West were the only two Hollywood leading ladies that never got to kiss their leading men. The studio brass thought that there was too much smoldering sexuality already without the smack of lip contact.

I used to date this Dutch man. The only thing I can remember about our time together is him saying, "Suck my tongue, suck it hard." I can't even remember his name, what he looked like, what his body or hair felt like in my hands, nothing. Nothing but that voice—probably not even his, but someone else's that I've replaced in my memory—telling me how to kiss him.

I have a friend who believes that the truth of love lies in the act of tongues. He refuses to kiss anyone unless he's positively sure that he's in love with that person. Once he's sure, he'd rather deep kiss than indulge in any fondling or anything ejaculatory. Once they kiss, once those lips touch, tongues slipped into the other's mouth, *Wham!* That's it, he wants the person to be his forever.

Aren't you placing inordinate power in a tongue? I once asked him. An act? An organ that ceases to work if you can't smell, if your nasal passages are blocked by allergies or bad sinuses? But he doesn't hear me, as he's busy thinking about someone he kissed four weeks ago. I hate to admit it, but sometimes I think he's right. When you kiss someone, it's the first taste of his mouth that will make or break your heart.

Acupuncturists believe that you can tell what ails the body by looking at the tongue. The coating of the tongue, how the tissue looks, how it hangs in your mouth, the cracks, the shape, how wet it is. Everything about the tongue points to something in your body. Every part of your body has some casual connection with your tongue.

I'm on the plane looking at the man beside me. I'm looking at his hands. Big, rough. There's some downy black hair on the back of his hands, on the flesh of the back of the fingers. He picks up the small airline muffin from his food tray, cuts it into thirds with the plastic knife, smears some spread on it, and brings it to his partner's mouth. He holds the piece between his thumb and middle finger, the second finger outstretched, ready to wipe the bit of crumb and butter off the side of his partner's lips. I stare at his hands through the whole trip. Two rings: a wedding band and a collegiate-looking pinkie ring, chunky with fake green gemstones looking like moss on gold. Hands, fingers to mouth, tongue. Along with a good smooch, I want a slice of tenderness.

"My love life (underline) (period) My love life is sometimes good (comma) sometimes bad (period) When it is good (comma) I am happy (period) When it is bad (comma) I feel sad (period)"

Inevitably, I find myself hanging out at Cafe Loveless, home of broken queer hearts. Warm coffee, warm soy milk, and warm draft beer, first refills free. The fridge broke down in 1986, the Half-and-Half ran out three years ago and never got replaced. You get to choose your coffee: Bitter Black or Diabetic Shock. Don't bother asking for an ashtray, there aren't any. Just tip your cigarette over the edge of the table; flick your ashes to the floor. Use your shoe to wipe it into the ground. You can request tango music, just ask the man behind the bar, but nobody feels like dancing much at Cafe Loveless. Just want to sit on the hard plastic chairs and nurse a warm coffee or warm beer, ashes underfoot, wanting to lick the spill off someone's fingertips. All dreaming of hot Fabio-like romance while the jukebox racks up the compact disc of Linda Rondstadt's greatest hits. *That'll be the day, when you say goodbye, that'll be the day…*

It's been so long since I've been in love with someone that is in love with me in return that I can't imagine the knowledge of knowing someone's body so intimately. How you can both be lying naked together on some lazy afternoon and you know where the soft and ticklish spots on the other body are, where the hard unfeeling parts crusted with dry dead skin are, where the hair is thick and luxurious, where it is soft, and where it is a scant fuzz.

These days I'm left to obsess about men that I chance across. An obsession is different from being smitten. One you want to know every detail about the prey, the other you just want to fill in the blanks with your fancy.

I'm trying to figure out what it is about this man that obsesses me. What it is that makes me think of him all the time, want to hear his voice, imagine him standing outside my door.

I love the way he moves: how his whole body, compact and sinewy, cuts through the air, determined and hard. I love his body hair: the way the stray strands of chest hair carelessly wisp out of the top of his T-shirt and curl in the hollow of his neck; how the hairs on his forearms mat down out of his rolled-up shirt sleeves, looking soft and shivery. I love the way he holds his cigarette, even though I am an avid nonsmoker, and I love the smell of stale cigarette smoke on his clothes. I love his tattoos. I love the way his ears feel. I love the way he leaves the smell of his body on my body, the taste of his tongue in my mouth.

Once I fell in love with an architect simply because I loved the fact that he makes buildings. Great big buildings. That such a small man made great structures out of steel and concrete that hold people and things up, pull them away from the ground, and hold them up to the scrutiny of air, gravity, and the elements.

I'm at the premiere of a really bad play that I cowrote. It's another one of those funny coincidences that there are all these men that I have had affairs with there, with their little nonthreatening boyfriends in tow. Well, I really wasn't having an affair with them, they were having an affair with me, which is a small but significant difference. At any rate, they were all trying to ignore me or else be very cordial and brief with me. Something about boyfriend being jealous, something about protecting their happy home lives: the whole idea of the two-bedroom-apartment-one-joint-vacation-a-year-let's-cook-together-darling lives. The red-light special at Relationships 'R' Us, open 24 hours, 365 days a year.

During the intermission, I think all their avoidance and their nervousness that I might say or do something to ruin their domestic bliss is quite funny. By the end of the play—and it is more dreadful than I thought it would be—I begin to see the pathetic nature of the whole setup.

Jealousy. They want to avoid the bugbear of jealousy.

I'm sitting at a café when a man—whom I once had sex with while he and his boyfriend were in the middle of yet another of their neverending undefined breakups—joins me. I haven't seen him in yonks and we chat a little, suggestions of a future tryst. He can't sit too long, boyfriend (they made up, apparently) may see us, he says. *Jealousy.*

"I thought you two had an open relationship," I say. His words are "modern relationship" or "modern couple," or something equally nauseatingly vague. "Doesn't matter, he'll still get jealous," he tells me.

You only get jealous because you want to be all things to the person you're smitten by or you think you're smitten by. Doesn't matter if you're not that thing or don't ever want to be that thing, you just want your sweetie to think that you are. And that's when you end up wearing stupid little tank tops and little cutoff shorts simply because your sweetie found some tramp attractive in them, never mind you look like some twitting idiot outside of your regular T-shirt and jeans ensemble that he first fell in love with you in. It's worse when it's not something physical like clothes or hair or body. Suddenly, you find yourself laughing different, moving different, method-acting. Yikes. The superior ones simply smack their sweeties on the head and develop an intense hatred toward their sweeties' obsessions. The inferior ones crumble.

Jealousy. All it takes is one chaste smooch to betray.

I used to date a man who was obsessed with the colour of the water in his toilet bowl. Blue. He wanted it to be as blue as possible. To achieve this, he resorted to dumping two or three of those blue-dyeing toilet bowl cleansers into the cistern every week. Once he even used dye, but that only stained the porcelain.

It really got to be an obsession. When he entered his house, the first thing he did was head straight for the bathroom and flush the bowl. He even brought the blue cleanser tablets when he went on a trip, just in case the hotel's toilet bowl didn't flush blue. Several times every night, he disentangled himself from our legs, arms, and the twisted sheets to go and flush the toilet.

All this was fine, but I guess I knew the relationship wouldn't work out, because I liked to piss in the bowl and watch the blue water turn green. I derived the same childish satisfaction as I did in all those years of high school chemistry laboratory, where I delighted in watching the liquids in the test tubes gradually precipitate and change colours in a glorious chemical reaction. Suddenly the most boring white powders would turn into a stunning cloudy crimson, or the bland milky liquid would hiss and spit gas and turn into a silver suspension floating in a thick greenish-yellow solution. Of course, I was supposed to be observing how the periodic table and the elements and compounds that make up this world we live in affect our lives, but damn, those colours!

Years later, I happened to see him on public-access television. He had his own show about psychic powers. (Come to think of it, he always did say he was psychic.) He was talking about spirit guides, those proverbial "little voices in your head," and how they talked to you. He asked the viewers to ask their spirit guides to tell them what colour he was thinking of in his head. I guessed blue. I was right.

Seeing him on that program and knowing that he was psychic made me feel so much better. At least now I know he knew that I wasn't going to return his phone calls. Still, in spite of his bizarre obsessions, he was really a rather sweet person. And he's also the first man out of many that I wish I had kissed goodbye properly.

Then there was this other guy, every time he got aroused his salivary glands kicked in and he would salivate like mad. This meant he always had to spit. He kept a little spittoon (it was a cheap wastebasket, really) with tissues wadded on the bottom beside his bed for this purpose. You would think it was quite gross, but actually he was a damn good kisser.

I knew a man I was dating was far too sensitive for me when he locked himself in the bathroom after I came home with various of my body parts pierced.

"Oh honey," he said through the locked door, his voice some kind of whimpering sob. "Piercing your body! But why? It's…it's such a random act of violence."

"Well, sweetie," I tried reasoning with him after I lured him out of the loo by lying about needing to shit real bad because of bad bacon. "It's hardly random. It's not like I was caught in a drive-by piercing."

Conventional wisdom has it that the most sensitive people are the best smoochers. This man was a horrid kisser actually: too much teeth, too little tongue, too much force. In this case, conventional wisdom and Newton's law of equal opposite reaction seemed to have betrayed me.

I'm trying to remember my first kiss but I can't.

Obsessions are best kept that way. It's really not wise

to try and bring them to you, even if you desperately want to. Even if you're horny beyond belief.

I discovered this with another obsession of mine. I met him quite by chance—the best way to meet anyone. For the week after our meeting, I kept saying his name over and over because I liked the way the syllables bumped into one another in my mind.

He works for a large chemical corporation but tells people that he is a photographer and a videomaker. He likes horror fiction, werewolves, vampires, that sort of thing. He writes short fiction and is on a gothic horror kick: Asylum doctor turns into an insect in a despicable plot by alien spiders trying to breed flies out of humans for consumption. He wants to take my picture, he tells me as we wait for the J-Church. He says I will end up looking Japanese when the picture comes out. I say no. He begs, says, "Please, please, I'll do anything, any-thing." I tell him no. "I don't like cameras," I say. He walks to the edge of the platform, turns around and says "Anything" one more time. He tells me how great the picture will look: half my face in shadows, half in a blinding light.

He gives me some of his writing to read. I wish he hadn't. I am not shocked by the writing at all. The improbability of it all does nothing to scare me. I tell him about Oliver Sacks's work, about how people are trapped for years inside a dead lifeless body, active minds stuck in a lifeless body, senses forced to watch everything change around them but powerless to feel or do anything. That's what scares me. He's unfamiliar with what I'm talking about. He gives me another piece. "It's unfinished," he says. "Help me find an ending."

Still, I love the way he says "I've got a brilliant idea" when something strikes his mind. I like the way I sound like him when I'm reading an unfamiliar text out loud. He's making a video about werewolves. On the streetcar he touches my chin, rubs the unshaven bits of fuzz and asks me if it was intentional. I say it's not. I rub his scant goatee too and he laughs. He tells me that he just recently had to change his aftershave, something about allergies causing blotches, and I remember the smell of his aftershave days ago when I leaned in to hug him goodbye. The smell of his aftershave mixed with the grimy smell of a workday. I get off the streetcar, cross the road, try not to look at him, but as the streetcar speeds by I see him through the plate glass of the back door, he's sitting with his legs up on the seat.

One night, I want to take him to Dolores Park, I want to sit him down in the middle of the park and I want to kiss him while the bats in the park are squealing because of the cold. Few people know that there are bats living in Dolores Park. I've lived around the park for two years. I didn't know myself. One day, I was walking past the park late at night to go to his place to pick up some papers and I heard the distinctive squeal of bats. Bats usually don't scream like that, the reference book in the library says. It must be the cold; they must be suffering.

One day I invite him over. We end up in my bedroom, where we start fooling around. It all would have been fine if I wasn't so conscious of the fact that I have carefully folded the manuscript he had given me to read into neat kindling and laid the entire script of 30-odd pages in my fireplace. The unburnt manuscript-kindling resting under the packed-woodchip log just hidden from his view by the dark fireplace screen and my houseguest periodically knocking on my door asking if I wanted a bacon and egg on white bread sandwich makes the entire tryst quite unsettling. That and his deformed left nipple.

As sexually liberated as I try to be, deformed nipples scare the shit out of me. I don't mind the severely pierced keloided ones because I know they were manipulated into such a state; but the ones that slant off to strange tangents all by themselves, aureoles that cave into dark nipples that look like large blackheads, those give me the heebie-jeebies.

Penises are a different matter, though. I quite enjoy deformed penises. This is probably because the first penises that I was attracted to and spent hours staring at and masturbating to were those in my father's medical books that he stored under my brother's bed.

Following the page numbers in the index, I was led to little shriveled diseased penises rotting through to the urethra, hanging bulbous members bloated to look like a fleshy tennis ball, and members dangling in semi-erection to show the world their horrible scabs and sores—all in fabulous colour.

Perhaps this prepared me for the first pierced penis that I ever saw. It was at a jack-off party and somehow it didn't faze me. In fact I found it quite erotic, and I thought it was a shame the bugger it was attached to was more interested in wanking off with someone else all evening. My companion, however, found the pierced dick quite unsettling, and his balls immediately retracted into his body and he had to escape to the kitchen to recompose himself.

He later told me that he was unable to have a full erection for days after witnessing that penis.

Once I had phone sex with a man. He had a very normal voice. Nothing exceptional. Tonal quality, inflection, phrasing—the kind of voice you hear on the street as you pass by two people chatting away or when the phone rings and it's someone you don't know, he gives you a name you don't remember and then tries to sell you investment information.

He wanted to be fucked in the arse without a condom, wanted to feel it *been so long, man, really need to feel that hot cock in me*. I made him shoot his first load on my dick, then fucked him up his arse using his jism as lubricant. After I came, I put my hand under his arse, palm up, he squeezed the collective cum and anal mucus out of his rectum noiselessly onto my waiting palm then jacked off another load into my hand. He used his tongue to mix the two, his watery jism and my denser congealed jism, into a swirl, and licked it off my hand, every single drop. When that was done, I wiped my hand on his face, pulled him to me, and kissed him hard on the mouth, sucking his tongue roughly.

I'm trying to remember my first good kiss but I can't.

I've had incredibly bad luck with demonic-looking men. Sure, I find them vastly attractive, but somehow they seem to be attracted to other demonic-looking men. I try to look demonic but it really doesn't work with me. The best I can do is look like the boy next door's younger brother, who lives beside the most gorgeous demonic-looking bloke.

The most erotic thing I have ever seen was this brilliantly demonic-looking man eating sushi with a metal fork. On anyone else, the sight would have been quite ridiculous, but on this one man it was enough to make me want to cook him breakfast for the rest of my life.

In my search for a demonic-looking lover, I tried placing a classified ad in the local newsweekly, but due to a typo I was surprised to discover that there are quite a sizable number of actual Satanists in San Francisco.

The other day as I was walking down the street I discovered a new fetish: Men with tattoos on the back of their necks. The back of a man's neck has always been the favourite part of man's body for me. This does get quite problematic, as I will often find myself getting quite aroused when I'm sitting behind a particularly sinewy neck on the bus or when the light from a cinema screen hits the side of a fuzzed neck in front of me.

Ah! The cinema. At a rescreening of Bertolucci's filmic recreation of Bowles's *The Sheltering Sky,* I flirted heavily with a man. Throughout the movie, I gave up Debra Winger's search for her sexual self for that man's neck and how it glowed in the flickering of the screen. After the screening, I was determined to try to pick him up. I tried to approach him but the crowds cut me off, and when I did reach the foyer all that was left of him was the tub of popcorn he was munching into and the Dixie cup of soda resting in the empty popcorn tub. One in the other, resting on the edge of the trash bin. Suddenly I was gripped with the urge to grab his trash and lick the tip of the straw, where his lips lingered during John Malkovich's tragic and pointless death. Fortunately, the cinema manager came by and tipped the cartons into the bin and stomped the trash down with his boot to flatten it, thus saving me from embarrassing myself with such an indecently obsessive act.

Now I find myself falling behind men on the street who have black squiggles peeking out the tops of the back of their shirts. And worse, I find myself longing to lean over and place my lips on the neck. Nothing else but lip to neck.

The act of kissing a person's neck is possibly the most sensual act known to humankind. The neck is the body's most vulnerable spot: muscle, nerves, and veins built around a vertebral column. In the animal kingdom, the smart mammals have been known to protect their necks vehemently; they never ever expose their necks unnecessarily. If you watch documentaries on hunters and the hunted, that's where lions bite deer and where lions bite each other. Never mind the little bit of flesh over the heart, there are ribs that protect it, but the neck—nothing.

The lips also are highly sensitive: something about all those blood vessels flowing so close to the surface and the close proximity to the tongue and all of its glands and sensory stuff.

There is a proper way to kiss someone on the neck. First, you must always start on the back or the side. Second, and this is the most important thing, you must never, never touch the other person with any other part of your body. Only lip to neck, nothing else. Let the neck feel only the press of warm lips and the lips feel the vast flesh of neck. When this happens, the microscopic space between lip and neck heats up vastly because air is a poor conductor of heat. It's kind of like how a blanket or an animal fluffing its fur works. You may be in the middle of the Sahara and you will still feel that one intense spot of heat surging out of your lover's lips and through your neck.

Smooch music: Sam Cooke, Marvin Gaye, the Supremes, Dusty in Memphis, Ella doing Gershwin, Ella with Ellington.

It's late and I can't sleep. It's been raining like mad and the roof is leaking everywhere. Drops of water sneak down the fireplace and drop like flies on the dead ashes. I have to keep my curtains drawn to trap the heat. That's fine, but when the wind blows, the leaves and branches of the palm tree outside my window scrape against the pane. It makes a hideous sound. I know if I can see the smack of the frond on the pane, it'll all be okay. But the curtains are drawn and I'm lying under three blankets and a sleeping bag trying not to move or I'll wake the damn cat curled up at the foot of the bed. I'm still trying to remember that first good kiss and the last good kiss and what happened in between, while Ella scats something fierce; and while my heart breaks again, Anna May Wong and Mae West are off somewhere holding each other's faces in their hands, teaching each other how to kiss.